# ALL FOR FREEDOM:

A True Story of Escape
from the Nazis

# ALL FOR FREEDOM

## A True Story of Escape from the Nazis

D. T. DAVIES
with
Ioan Wyn Evans

Gomer

To my wife Beti,
rock of ages.

Published in 2016 by
Gomer Press, Llandysul, Ceredigion, SA44 4JL

ISBN 978 1 78562 168 0

A CIP record for this title is available from the British Library.

© D. T. Davies 2016

D. T. Davies asserts his moral right under the
Copyright, Designs and Patents Act 1988
to be identified as the author of this work.

All rights reserved. No part of this book may be reproduced,
stored in a retrieval system, or transmitted in any form
or by any means, electronic, electrostatic, magnetic tape, mechanical,
photocopying, recording or otherwise without permission
in writing from the above publishers.

This book is published with the financial support of the
Welsh Books Council.

Printed and bound in Wales at
Gomer Press, Llandysul, Ceredigion
www.gomer.co.uk

# If

If you can keep your head when all about you
    Are losing theirs and blaming it on you,
If you can trust yourself when all men doubt you,
    But make allowance for their doubting too;
If you can wait and not be tired by waiting,
    Or being lied about, don't deal in lies,
Or being hated, don't give way to hating,
    And yet don't look too good, nor talk too wise:

If you can dream – and not make dreams your master;
    If you can think – and not make thoughts your aim;
If you can meet with Triumph and Disaster
    And treat those two impostors just the same;
If you can bear to hear the truth you've spoken
    Twisted by knaves to make a trap for fools,
Or watch the things you gave your life to, broken,
    And stoop and build 'em up with worn-out tools:

If you can make one heap of all your winnings
    And risk it on one turn of pitch-and-toss,
And lose, and start again at your beginnings
    And never breathe a word about your loss;
If you can force your heart and nerve and sinew
    To serve your turn long after they are gone,
And so hold on when there is nothing in you
    Except the Will which says to them: 'Hold on!'

If you can talk with crowds and keep your virtue,
    Or walk with Kings – nor lose the common touch,
If neither foes nor loving friends can hurt you,
    If all men count with you, but none too much;
If you can fill the unforgiving minute
    With sixty seconds' worth of distance run,
Yours is the Earth and everything that's in it,
    And – which is more – you'll be a Man, my son!

                                    Rudyard Kipling

## Acknowledgements

When I returned home in 1944 I met a former soldier who had served in the Army of Occupation following the First World War. He began to question me about my time in the army. After I had recounted some of my wartime experiences as a prisoner of war under the Nazis, he turned to me and said, 'I don't believe a word of it. I always found the Germans to be kind and friendly, so much so that I came close to marrying a German woman.' Following that reaction, I didn't talk about my time as a POW for years on end, not even to my family.

When I reached my 90s, my sons insisted I put my experiences on paper for the sake of my two grandsons and five granddaughters.

But where would I begin? Michael, Graham and Andrew decided to take me on a journey to Austria, to revisit some of the places I'd been as a prisoner of war. Consequently, that journey was filmed for a television programme on my wartime experiences, *Heb Ryddid, Heb Ddim* ('Without Freedom, We Have Nothing'), produced by Ioan Wyn Evans. After the programme was broadcast, I was urged by many to relate the full story in a book.

It wasn't easy to remember every detail, particularly the sad and emotional occasions. But, the book has seen the light of day through Ioan's perseverance and incredible patience, and as a family we thank him sincerely.

I'd like to thank Beti and the family for their constant support at all times. Thanks to Paul London from New Zealand for his help and research on the family of Roy Natusch, and for providing me with pictures of Roy and Sammy Hoare. I'm also grateful to him for contacting Norman McLean's family so that his picture could be included too. Paul also put me in contact with Tyler Bridges, Dick Bridges' son, who gave me pictures of his father and his fellow American, Glenn Loveland. Tyler is writing a book about his late father and has travelled to Hungary and Serbia to verify facts. Thanks to all the families for their kind support and co-operation.

Graham, my son, has visited Belgrade and had a warm welcome when he enquired about Otto, whom I got to know in Yugoslavia, and who lectured at Belgrade University. During his visit, Graham was taken to some of the places mentioned in this book, and visited the Partisan monument at Fruśka Gora.

And, finally, thanks to Ceri Wyn Jones and Gomer Press for their excellent work.

'Freedom is the foundation for peace'.

D.T. Davies,<br>
Dryslwyn,<br>
Carmarthenshire.

# Contents

| | |
|---|---|
| Foreword | 11 |
| A Call to Arms | 13 |
| In the Beginning | 22 |
| Foreign Fields | 27 |
| The Battle | 37 |
| Behind the Wire | 51 |
| Hard Labour | 59 |
| Back to the Stalag | 69 |
| The Big Chance | 73 |
| On the Run | 83 |
| Behind Bars | 91 |
| 'Top Secret' Plans | 100 |
| Hell on Earth | 107 |
| Following the Red Star | 116 |
| Bullets and Screams | 122 |
| A Flight to Freedom | 129 |
| Home Again | 138 |
| Past and Present | 146 |
| Crete Once More | 152 |
| Lessons Learned? | 157 |

## Foreword

There are some words which are used far too frequently. One such word is 'hero'. Every day we hear about 'heroes' of all kinds, whether they be a football hero, a pop hero, or a film hero. But what really makes a hero?

A few years ago I met a man called David Tom Davies, or D.T. Davies. For decades, 'DT', as he is known in his home county of Carmarthenshire, had been at the forefront of local government politics. A democrat by nature, he had been chairman of Carmarthenshire and Dyfed county councils. He was well known as a principled fighter for the interests of his constituents, and he did so with enthusiasm and vitality, but with great humility as well.

But, 75 years ago, D.T. Davies was fighting on a very different front. In 1941, whilst serving in the Royal Artillery during the Second World War, he was captured by the German army and became a prisoner of war. He spent three years at different prison camps in central and eastern Europe. He witnessed dark deeds. But, all the while, one thing kept him going – the urge to escape.

His is an amazing and uplifting story. It is the tale of one man's fight for a basic human right – freedom – against a backdrop of unimaginable cruelty and suffering. For his bravery, he was awarded the Military Medal.

D.T. Davies is now in his late 90s, and 70 years after the end of the war, he recounts his incredible experiences.

It was an honour to work with DT on this book, and accompany him on a journey through his past, sometimes revisiting difficult places and horrendous scenes, but also hearing about the support shown by ordinary people who had kindness in their hearts.

Whatever your views on war, D.T. Davies's courage, determination and humility should be highlighted and respected. This is the story of a man who truly deserves to be called a 'hero'.

Ioan Wyn Evans<br>Carmarthen

# A Call to Arms

They were hard times. The great economic depression had dominated life in 1930s rural Wales. But by 1939 it seemed things were getting better, at last. My 21st birthday was looming, and I knew a letter would soon arrive in the post. I knew as well that the message would hardly be a birthday greeting.

Although we weren't at war, the government had passed an act enforcing young men to join the armed forces once they reached their 21st year. It was a statutory period of military training we all had to endure over six months. At the time I worked as an office clerk in Llandeilo, Carmarthenshire. And to be honest it wasn't a job I enjoyed at all. So, when the letter arrived calling me for a medical, before being enlisted for the army, I looked upon it as an opportunity. It was a chance to inject a bit of excitement into life after a difficult decade. I was hoping a period of adventure lay ahead.

A month later I was on a train to Kinmel Park, near Rhyl in Denbighshire, North Wales. That's where we were going to be based for the training. Five of us went up from Llandeilo. Doug James was from New Road and Richard Williams was the son of a well-known local solicitor, Hugh

Williams. Then there was Llew Jones, a carpenter from nearby Pen-y-banc, along with Reg Thomas who, like me, came from the village of Dryslwyn.

Our train was jam-packed with boys from all over west Wales, from places like Llanelli, Ammanford and Llandybie. And I remember meeting a young man from Brynaman, as well. He was Jack Davies and it was the beginning of a long friendship. After the war, Jack went on to be an agent for the Labour politician, James ('Jim') Griffiths, who became the first Secretary of State for Wales. And decades later, Jack and I would become colleagues as fellow councillors on Dyfed County Council.

When we reached our training post at Kinmel Park, we were frogmarched to a large tent. There they took all our names, and we were each given a personal army number. It was drummed in to us that this was a number we had to remember, at all costs. And mine is still with me to this day – 1492720. The officers rarely used the full number, however. They'd refer to us by our surnames and the last three digits of our personal numbers. So I was Davies 720.

If we were hoping for home comforts, we had plainly come to the wrong place. We were split into groups of eight, given some poles and a large piece of canvas, and told to go away and erect a tent. For the next six months, that tent was going to be our home. We would be sleeping on the floor on some bags of hay which could at best be described as makeshift mattresses. It was all pretty basic.

Within a few days, we were given our uniforms. What a pantomime! We waited in long queues for what seemed like hours to get our breeches and our greatcoats, all First World War-issue. The scene was a picture of chaos. We were asked our measurements and which were thrown our clothes, most of which was either too large or too small for us. This sparked a mass bartering session as we tried to swap clothing, hoping we'd get something which would be a half-decent fit, at least.

The breeches posed the greatest problem. If they were too tight, you couldn't walk. But if they weren't tight enough, they'd fall down. Most of us looked a mess, to be honest. It was all a bit of a shambles, and the early indications didn't bode well for the months ahead. But we had to laugh, and we did.

Worse was to follow in the form of vaccinations. I think we were given three injections in all, though I can't remember for what. But I do recall the needles very clearly. They were huge. Big enough to scare horses. Some boys collapsed like a sack of potatoes when they saw the size of these needles. Luckily, things were pretty straightforward for me. But I do remember being told to run round a large courtyard for several laps after being vaccinated. We needed to pump our arms, they said, so that the vaccine circulated throughout the body. I woke up the morning after with a stiff and heavy arm, and I was aching from head to toe. But there was no long-term damage, and within a day or two everything was back to normal.

We had been at Kinmel Park a while before they trusted us to wield weapons. Then, as if from nowhere, rifles appeared. The subject of the first lesson was how to take aim, but the technical skills of some of the would-be soldiers left quite a bit to be desired. Indeed, so off target were some of the not-so-sharpshooting recruits that the others were often forced to literally run for cover.

Within a few weeks, we were given the responsibility of guarding the camp. Why we were guarding the camp was not immediately clear to us: after all, the equipment we had was hardly modern and up-to-date. Anyway, four of us were summoned for duty. And to defend ourselves we were each given a pickaxe handle. The combined armoury to secure the camp against potential enemy attack was, therefore, four pickaxe handles! If those bungling soldiers on *Dad's Army* were a model of incompetence, we were in a different league again! We didn't know whether to laugh or cry.

It wasn't long before we progressed from rifles to the bigger guns. Huge, heavy and old, these things again dated back to the First World War. We had only been using them for a week or so when the officers informed us that it was time for us to start using searchlights in our exercises. We would then be properly equipped to look out for potential enemy planes making night-time raids. The officers obviously thought we were becoming quite adept at using these searchlights, which were powered by diesel engines, because one day we were informed, 'We're going to have a proper practice soon, chaps. We'll have a real aeroplane coming over, so make sure you can spot it with those lights.'

The big night arrived. As the barracks bell rang, we all rushed out. But by the time we got the searchlight up and running, the aeroplane had passed. It was another comic moment underlining how inept, how shapeless (as we like to say in rural Wales), it all was. There was no real organisation or leadership from the officers and, consequently, we, the conscripted soldiers, had no idea what we were doing.

Our marching exercises also confirmed this. The man (the very short man, as I remember) who taught us had been a Major in the First World War. He ordered the smallest men to the front and the tallest to the back, and expected everyone to march at exactly the same pace. It hadn't occurred to him that the taller men had longer strides than the shorter men, so walking at the same speed, particularly wearing our ill-fitting breeches, and carrying rifles on our backs, proved a challenge and a half!

After we'd walked about half a mile, the miniature Major shouted, 'Halt! About turn!' Then we turned round. Now the short men had to keep up with the taller men, some almost sprinting to match the longer strides in front. What a sight! It was an absolute farce.

It was the same major who once gave us some very strange instructions when we were out marching. 'If a plane comes now I want you men to throw yourselves to the side,' he said. 'Then I want you to shoot at the plane; that way we may be able to take it down...' We all looked at one another, each of us thinking how on earth this was going to happen. We had no bullets in our rifles. So, there we were, grown men, shooting at a plane with imaginary ammunition, as if our lives depended on it. Incredible!

For the first few weeks at Kinmel Park, we didn't have any vehicles at the camp. Then, out of the blue, a dozen or more cars appeared on the parade ground, and one of the officers shouted, 'How many of you can drive?' Only two hands went up: Jackie Boast's and mine. Jackie was from Pontardawe in the Swansea valley, and we had, unbeknown to us, just volunteered to teach the rest of the boys to drive. And, as we soon found out, most of them had never sat behind the wheel of a car before.

Jackie and I were given the use of two large army lorries. The biggest snag was that they didn't have any windscreens, and as north-east Wales isn't known for its tropical climate, that wasn't something we greeted with too much joy. But, there was a job to do, and we cracked on with it. Even in those days the roads in that area were quite busy. So the sight of our big heavy trucks holding up the traffic didn't go down well with other drivers. Even the buses sped past us.

Some of my fellow conscripts took advantage of my ability to drive. One day I was approached by a group who wanted me to drive them into nearby Rhyl for a night out. They told me a local publican had lent them a car for the evening, but they needed a driver. In a moment of weakness I agreed to do the job. Everything went fine, and we got back to the camp before curfew time.

Next morning, on my way to the parade ground, I saw a car similar to the one I had driven the night before, an identical car, in fact. On closer inspection, I soon realised it was the actual same car! It wasn't owned by a local publican at all but belonged to someone who worked at the barracks, someone who certainly hadn't given his permission for it to be used as a taxi! Apparently one of the boys had somehow managed to get hold of the keys, so when I next saw the ringleader of the crew I had driven into Rhyl, I told him, 'You do that to me again, and I will kick your arse!' We both looked at each other and laughed, but I never drove them into town again.

After a few weeks I'd got to know a few of the boys quite well, and some of us would meet regularly during the summer nights to have a chat and a laugh. It was also a chance to enjoy some entertainment. Some of us would do a turn or two in Welsh, whilst others would sing or recite something in English.

One bank holiday a huge marquee was erected near the entrance to the camp: an evening of entertainment had been scheduled and invitations had gone out to all the conscripts' families. This was fine for those who lived in North Wales or Liverpool or Manchester, but for those like me from south-west Wales, the chances of our families popping up to see us were slim, at best. The journey from Carmarthenshire to Denbighshire in those days was like a voyage to the moon.

During our preparations for the big event, one officer had managed to get hold of a piano from somewhere, and he approached me with a request. 'Davies 720,' he said. 'Get some of these Welsh chaps together and see if we can have a sing-song.'

I've always loved singing, and I can make a lot of noise, but I'm not musical in any way. And I tried telling the officer that. It didn't seem to cut any ice, and his reply was, 'Don't worry, Davies, just get the men together – as many as you can, old boy.'

I managed to get a gang of 20 or so together. The next challenge was finding someone to play the piano. Could any one play? Heads were shaken all round, until one of the boys admitted that he could play 'a little bit, but only hymns'. Given our predicament, that was good enough. So, we decided to sing the classic Welsh hymn, 'Calon Lân' – and we got two encores. The audience loved us, so it is unlikely that they were music aficionados! And to be honest I think that moment signalled the peak of the musical careers of most if not all of us.

I got on quite well with our Captain, an affable Scot who had played rugby for his country. On one occasion he'd asked me to arrange a team of Welsh soldiers to play in an inter-nations tournament. I can't remember much about the games, but I do recall that they were a lot of fun. In time, the Captain asked me if I was interested in putting my name forward for promotion, so that I could become an officer. I was flattered. Three of us were shortlisted for interviews held in Chester. The other two were both privately-educated Englishmen. My background was very different.

A member of the interview panel asked, 'Tell us, Davies, what does your father do?' I answered nervously, 'He's a miner, sir.' The officer's response was suitably underwhelming: 'Oh right, yes.' Very soon afterwards the brief interview came to an end.

I didn't get the promotion. Later the Captain who'd put my name forward asked how the interview had gone. I told him the panel had enquired about my father's occupation, and that I'd said he was a miner. 'You bloody fool,' said the Captain. 'You should have told them that he owned the bloody mine!'

Every Sunday we would go to the beautiful church at Bodelwyddan, a truly inspirational building. One morning in September 1939, however, we heard that we had to attend a special church parade. We couldn't work out why. Even more mysteriously we saw one of the officers carrying a wireless. We were ordered to gather round and listen to a broadcast on the airwaves.

At 11 o'clock, the Prime Minister, Neville Chamberlain, addressed the people. Everyone was gripped. No one dared move. He announced that German forces had entered Poland, before uttering the words none of us would forget, 'I have to tell you now... this country is at war with Germany.'

There was silence. No one said a word. We all knew now that the war had officially begun. The fun and farce of the training camp was well and truly over. It was serious businesss now, and we knew we wouldn't be going home any time soon.

# In the Beginning

Llandybie, Carmarthenshire, where agriculture and the coal industry co-existed happily, is where it all began. In July 1918, I arrived in the world as the first son of James and Martha Davies, who had married a year earlier. I was, it seems, a determined soul. So much so, that according to family folklore, the Kaiser decided to concede defeat in the First World War once he'd understood that I had appeared on the scene!

My family roots were firmly in the fertile fields of the Tywi valley. My father's people hailed from the parish of Llanegwad, whilst my mother's were from neighbouring Llangathen. Several generations had passed since the Davies family had lived in Llanegwad parish: many of the family had apparently left for America and the opportunities of the 'new world'. But it was the pull of the old world that drew my father back, and he decided that he wanted to raise his young family in the parish of his forefathers. So, that's how we ended up in the village of Dryslwyn, halfway between Carmarthen and Llandeilo. I was five years old when we arrived there, and I've lived there ever since: it is the place I have proudly called 'home' for over 90 years.

Although my father, James, lived in Carmarthenshire

when he first met my mother, he wasn't actually born and raised in the county. He was from the old iron industry heartland of Merthyr Tydfil. Diminutive in stature, he was a very able boy who had succeeded in getting a place at the local grammar school. His father, William Davies, was an influential figure at one of Merthyr's Methodist chapels, and wanted his son to become a minister. But my father wasn't at all keen: he had career ambitions of his own. He had decided that his future lay underground, no doubt influenced by the fact that a relative of my grandmother's (my father's mother) owned several collieries. Such was the subsequent disagreement between my father and his father that Dad ended up leaving home and heading for the Ammanford area to work in the mines. That's where he met Mam.

My father was very keen on music and singing. I wouldn't say he had a great voice, but he understood the art and was quite an expert on tonic sol-fa, the sight-reading system which was extremely popular in Welsh nonconformist chapels.

My father may not have wanted to pursue a career in the pulpit, but he was still genuinely interested in religion, and while the rest of our family attended the local church services, Dad remained a Methodist to the core. He was an amiable man, but he would sometimes get involved in heated debates, sparked by scriptural discussions. Although I didn't inherit my father's interest in religion, I've no doubt that his spirit and determination did rub off on me.

Martha, my mother, was a kind and gentle woman, who always strove to do her very best for her children. Like most women of her time, she was primarily a homemaker. Life was tough for working-class families such as ours, but we didn't really want for anything. We had food, clothing and boots on our feet. And we were happy.

I was the eldest of four children. I had two brothers, Islwyn and Gwynfor, and a sister, Iona, of whom only Gwynfor survives.

We all attended Cwrt Henri School, near Dryslwyn, where I did quite well and managed to secure a place at Llandeilo Grammar School. I was reasonably successful there as well, and was very keen on chemistry in particular. I even had dreams of staying on at school, and perhaps going to university.

My father's health wasn't good, however. Like many miners, he suffered from pneumoconiosis, a severe chest condition brought on by years of working underground. When I was at grammar school, it worsened considerably. I knew I couldn't carry on with my studies, and that I needed to leave school to try to find work to help support my family.

The chemistry teacher came over to our house to try to persuade my parents to let me stay on at school, so that I could realise my dream of going to university. But in fairness to my parents, like hundreds of other families at the time, they really couldn't afford to do that. So, I left school and made my way out into the big wide world.

It wasn't a good time to be looking for work: the economic depression of the 1930s was biting hard. But I was determined to get a job. I had never been afraid of hard work, after all, and was always ready to roll up my sleeves. So I accepted all offers of work, mostly agricultural labouring jobs, a few days here and there, wherever and whenever farmers wanted help.

I was also given a job by Mr Bryer, owner of the village garage, working on his lorries mostly. Then I got some shifts as a postman, covering the full-time posties when they were away on holidays. I became a jack of all trades, and every penny was welcomed. It was that kind of era. We just had to make the best of the little we had.

A little later a friend of mine told me he was leaving his post as an office clerk in Llandeilo, and suggested I should apply for his job. Working in the confines of an office didn't really appeal to me. But, it was a full-time position with a wage to match, so I decided to go for it. I got the job, and though I was never really happy there, I remained in post until I was called up for my army training.

When I reflect on my childhood, I can see how much store was placed on being true to oneself. If we gave our word, we had to keep to it. There was no turning back. We were also taught to treat everyone fairly, whoever they were, or whatever they did. In 1930s rural Carmarthenshire stepping out of line, or getting above one's station, were not acceptable traits. People who did things like that were usually given a short, sharp shock. They were reminded of who they were and where they'd come from. It was all about doing the right thing, whatever the circumstances were – and those values I was taught as a child have remained with me throughout my life. They were values, however, that would be severely tested.

# Foreign Fields

Soon after the outbreak of war was announced, I was told I was going to be sent to France. All the others who had trained with me were going somewhere else, and why I had been singled out for preferential treatment remains a mystery to this day. So it was that I found myself in Cherbourg, Normandy, on the north-west coast of France, where I was told to stay to await further instructions. It was the winter of 1939 and we were kept in the dark about what lay ahead. Looking back now and knowing how things turned out, maybe that wasn't such a bad thing.

About ten of us had been gathered together, all from the same regiment, the Royal Artillery, but all from different batteries. I didn't know any of the others, and was left wondering, 'What's happening here? Where are we supposed to go? Why all this mystery?' Then, out of the blue, we were all given a small parcel of food, and told to jump on a train. After what must have been the best part of two days on the train, we finally arrived at Marseille, in the south of France. There we received our next instruction: we were to board a ship, which was already waiting for us in the port.

The sea looked calm and tranquil. There seemed to

be no wild waves or choppy waters but, boy, was I ill! I was as sick as the proverbial dog. Some relief came when we reached the shores of Malta in the heart of the Mediterranean Sea, nestled between the Italian island of Sicily and North Africa. But the bad news was that we had to stay on the ship. We were aiming for Alexandria in Egypt, before going on to Suez and the canal linking the Mediterranean and the Red Sea.

Soon after we arrived, we met the engineers who'd come to erect a searchlight. Their colonel had come to meet us as well. His message to us was most matter of fact. 'You boys are only in the army for six months,' he said tersely. 'It doesn't matter how good you are, there'll be no promotion for you. The soldiers we have here are full-time professionals – they'll be the ones who are promoted.' We weren't too bothered by this, to be honest: we were young and inexperienced, and weren't harbouring deep ambitions of promotion at this point.

What did concern us, though, was that, with January 1940 approaching, our six-month period of training was coming to an end. What was actually going to happen to us at the end of that time? There was no mention at all of sending us home. So, one of the boys stood up and asked the Colonel if we were going to be sent back to Britain shortly. The question didn't go down well. 'The war has started, man,' grunted the Colonel. 'We can't let you go yet!' And at that point we all had the feeling that this was going to be a long old haul. The lush green fields of Carmarthenshire seemed further away than ever.

The first few weeks in Egypt flew by, though. There were quite a few things to learn. There was Morse Code to begin with, not to mention getting used to handling the big guns and the heavy artillery. The shells weighed 100 pounds apiece and as part of our training, we were expected to lift x number of those in a minute. So we had to be physically strong. And because we trained so hard, we – the amateur rabble – became better at our duties than the proper professional soldiers. That gave us a real lift, but the pros weren't too happy. Still, there's nothing like a bit of good old-fashioned competition, is there?

After we'd been in Egypt for a while, one of the officers asked if any of us could drive. As I had at Kinmel Park, I put my hand up straightaway. This time I was the only one, and, as a result, there was a job waiting for me. I was summoned to go to Cairo with the engineers to pick up a vehicle to bring back to Suez. So off we went, two warrant officers in the front and me in the back. They didn't say a word to me throughout the journey. Not a word. No doubt they were trying to assert their superiority.

When we arrived in Cairo, they just left me there – with no food and no instructions. I was left to fend for myself as if it were some kind of initiative test. What was I supposed to do next? I went to a local British Army office and explained my predicament. I was told I was in the wrong place, but they didn't tell me where the right place was! They were friendly enough, however: they gave me some food and told me I could go to sleep in one of the sheds they had nearby. I was the only one there.

When I woke up the next morning, I was told that someone from the nearby town of Heliopolis was on his way to meet me. He was going to bring a lorry for me to take back to Suez, a journey of about 80 miles. Like Cairo itself, all of this was new to me, so I decided that the only way to approach it was to treat it as an adventure, and hope that I would get back to Suez without too many hiccups.

Anyway, the chap arrived from Heliopolis. Brandishing some kind of checklist, he declared that the truck was ready, but I don't think he had the first idea what he was talking about. But the lorry was filled with petrol, and that was good enough for me. I was ready to hit the road.

Next morning I left Cairo first thing. Luckily, I found my way out, without too many problems, and I was on my way. Blessed with good fortune on a tricky journey, I reached Suez safely. Once I got back I was told I'd been given another task: to teach some of the professional soldiers to drive – a heady job indeed for a raw recruit from rural Wales.

My ability to drive gave me some freedom and variety that wasn't afforded to most of my colleagues. One morning I was told that I was to drive the Colonel to Cairo for a three-day trip. That meant I had an opportunity to explore the ancient city as the Colonel attended to his business. Whilst I was out wandering the city, I bumped in to another soldier who was there enjoying a brief period of leave. We struck a conversation, got on well, and decided to proceed with our city tour together.

We headed for the world-famous landmarks of the

Pyramids and the Sphinx. There we got chatting to three other British soldiers, junior officers, all three of whom were real characters, who enjoyed a laugh and a joke. I'm still not sure how they did it, but somehow they managed to get hold of a horse each for us to ride. What an experience that was! Once we got on, the horses bolted and began chasing one another. We had very little control over them: it was all we could do to hold on, let alone hold them back. But it was all good fun, and luckily, we were none the worse for it.

In the evening we were invited to dine with the three officers. As a rule of course, officers and common soldiers like us – the Privates and Gunners – were kept very much apart. There was no socialising between the ranks. But, these three were very different, and protocol was well and truly thrown out of the window. As far as they were concerned, how we got on was more important than who we were. It was a breath of fresh air to be in their company. One of them asked me what I did in the army. I explained and pointed out that my main role now seemed to be that of a driver. They told me they needed a driver and that I should request a transfer to join their regiment. I would have more adventures with them, they claimed.

When I got back to our base at the end of the three-day trip, I submitted my request for a transfer. Almost immediately, I was called in to see the Colonel. I could see he wasn't impressed. 'Why do you want a transfer, Davies?' he asked brusquely. I said I felt that I just wanted a change, and to experience new challenges elsewhere.

'There is nothing wrong with this regiment, Davies,' was the curt reply. 'If you stay here, you'll go back home alive. This is the safest place you'll find,' said the Colonel. Looking back now, he was probably right. But, at the time, I was an eager young soldier looking for adventure, seeking something more exciting than a quiet life.

A couple of months went by and the Colonel called me in to see him again. 'I've got something for you, Davies,' he said. 'You're going up to Port Said.' That was right at the mouth of the canal, about 100 miles from Suez. We were going to be erecting a searchlight there, right at the far end of the pier.

Once I got there I knew that there was some hard graft ahead of us. There was a lot of heavy lifting work, and it was done by hand. There wasn't a machine in sight. But they were good times. On the ground, our work was overseen by a Sergeant who shared my surname. Though he claimed to have Welsh roots, Sergeant Joe Davies was a straight-talking Yorkshireman. But he was a fair man, and you knew where you stood with him. He was a man I liked and respected.

Whilst we were in Port Said, the call went out for anyone with motorcycling experience. Again, I volunteered. And within minutes, I was a dispatch rider. Over the next few weeks I would travel regularly on the ferry from Port Fuad to Port Said and to a nearby aerodrome, mostly relaying messages back and forth.

It was on one of my journeys to the aerodrome that I took a tumble on a patch of road which crossed a rail track.

The young soldier at Kinmel Park in 1939: who knows what lies ahead for me?

Calm before the storm: the Sinai desert, Egypt, 1941. I'm the one on the right.

Stalag 18A outside Wolfsberg in Austria. The whole camp reeked of death. The thought of escape was the only thing which sustained me whilst I was there.

*Photo: Tanya O'Kennedy and Ian Brown, Stalag18a.org.uk*

The Russian prisoners at Stalag 18A. They were treated shamefully by the Nazi officers at the camp, dozens of them dying every week.

*Photos: Mike Riddle and Ian Brown, Stalag18a.org.uk*

Stadl an der Mur, Austria. Geoff Hallett (left), Dougie Arthur and me (right).

Murau, Austria. Len Caulfield (left), and Geoff Hallett from Cardiff either side of me.

Murau. The work was hard and the weather cold, but we were given a warm welcome.

Men of Murau. I'm standing next to Franz Moshammer (right), whilst the flat-capped man in the middle is station manager Ferdinand Zeiper, who always treated us fairly.

The moustached gentleman with me in Murau is the kind-hearted Franz Moshammer.

Dougie Arthur and Geoff Hallett, two good friends in Murau.

Wrapped up warm in the snow.

Roy Natusch from New Zealand, a remarkable man, indeed. He and I spent weeks on end planning our escape from Austria to Hungary.

Roy Natusch proudly displaying his medals. He died in 2009, aged 90.

A well-deserved break from our toils at Murau. I'm sitting between an Australian soldier (left) and Len Caulfield.

Joe Walker (left) and me. Joe escaped from Gaas in Austria with Roy Natusch and me. We crossed the border to Hungary before we were caught in woodland.

Agnes Kraller, owner of the farm where I worked when I escaped from Austria to Hungary.

Agnes Kraller and her family on the farm.

*Photos courtesy of the Kraller family*

Szigetvár, Hungary, in early 1944. It was like the United Nations there, but I was the sole Welshman (fourth from the left, middle row)!

Allen Hugh 'Sammy' Hoare from New Zealand.

Sammy Hoare and his wife. Sammy and I experienced Szigetvár, Hungary, and Yugoslavia together.

I hit some lurking sandbags and my motorbike overturned and slid, damaging part of the track in the process. We were always told not to stop if we hit anything. So, I just got back on the bike and kept on going. No one was hurt, even if my ego and I had collected the odd bruise!

Being in Egypt in 1940 was a strange experience. We were part of the war, yet we were far removed from it. I saw no actual military combat whilst I was there. Indeed, there were times when we were allowed to relax away from our day-to-day duties. On one such occasion a large group of us went for a day to the seaside. I was on the beach, ready to go for a swim, when I spotted someone in the sea. I couldn't believe my eyes. Standing waist-high in the waves was a familiar face. His name was Aneurin Lewis. And he lived in the same village as me back home in Carmarthenshire. He was out in Egypt on the anti-aircraft guns, but neither of us knew before that day that the other was in North Africa. After we'd got over the shock of seeing each other, I asked him what he was doing, because he looked as if he'd been searching for something. Then he looked at me somewhat coyly and said, 'Well, to be honest with you, Dai, I've just lost my false teeth.'

We both burst out laughing, before I tried lending him a helping hand in his dental quest in the Mediterranean. You couldn't have made it up: two young men from Dryslwyn looking for a pair of false teeth in the sea in Egypt. Anyway, despite our valiant efforts, we couldn't find the missing dentures. But it was a day I will never forget.

More aquatic antics lay ahead, however. When I was

stationed at Suez, we had an officer who had represented Cambridge University in the Boat Race, and he wanted to start a rowing team for the soldiers. It sounded like a good idea to me, though, admittedly, I had never actually rowed before. As it turned out, and if you pardon the pun, most of my team-mates were in the same boat! With little or no previous rowing experience, we all had to learn new techniques and terminology. We were granted special permission to use the canal, where we would usually row about a mile out and back, making smooth if steady progress. One day, however, things didn't go quite according to plan.

We were rowing as usual, a team of eight seemingly in tandem. Then, all of a sudden, our cox screamed loudly. Facing the opposite direction, the oarsmen couldn't see the problem, of course, which may well have been a good thing, because judging by the cox's demeanour, whatever it was, it was a terrifying sight. It turns out that it was a ferry boat and we were rowing, unbeknown to us, towards a head-on collision with this huge craft. The pitch of the cox's voice rose higher and higher. 'Oars, oars,' he shrieked, begging us to slow down. We stopped rowing and, in the nick of time, our boat ground to a bobbing halt a few yards short of the course of the oncoming craft. And the ferry boat passed serenely by! It was one hell of a close shave: the look on the cox's face told us how close we had been to a crash which would have been fatal for us all. I'm sure he had seen his life flash before him. Significantly, that was the last time any of us rowed on the canal.

My time at Port Said grew more eventful by the day. Shortly after the rowing debacle we were bombed for the first time, by Italian aeroplanes, but because they flew so high above us, their bombs were dispersed over a wide area, and, fortunately for us, they weren't particularly well-targeted, and no one was hurt.

Italian bombers weren't the only airborne enemy to attack us in Egypt, by the way. This was no man-made threat, but its bite caused untold havoc. It was the mosquito and, after I was bitten by one, I caught malaria for the first time. It was an illness whose effects would plague me for years to come.

On a day-to-day basis, most of my time was taken up with driving duties, like the time I was commissioned to go to meet soldiers from the Black Watch, the Royal Highland Regiment, who were making their way over from Palestine. Some were to come back with us to Port Said, and others were on their way to Ismailia, to the west of Suez. I was accompanied in the truck by one of the officers, Second Lieutenant Jones. Some way into the journey he told me to stop. He was intent on riding a motorcycle we had in the back of the truck. This was the middle of the desert. There were no designated roads, only tracks of sand. This was dangerous terrain. So I told him that I couldn't allow him to do this because I was in charge of the motorcycle, and I didn't think it was safe to ride it in such conditions.

I could see from his face that my opinion counted for nothing. What is more, it wasn't an opinion I should have voiced. 'I'm the senior officer here, Davies,' he told me, pulling rank. 'You do what I tell you.' And that was it. Such was the army's hierarchical structure, I had no real choice in the matter. I had to obey his orders.

So, we stopped immediately. Second Lieutenant Jones fetched the bike from the back of the truck, and off he went. Within a few hundred yards, he was regretting his decision. He hit some kind of hole in the sand, and off the bike he came, with an almighty thud. He did manage to get back on, but his pride was well and truly hurt, and judging by his reduced speed, I think he'd learnt his lesson as well. I must confess to feeling a quiet sense of satisfaction.

In November 1940, having been in Egypt for nearly a year, some of us were told that it was now time to move on. We were heading for Crete. Little did I know at the time that what lay ahead would determine my future for the rest of the war and beyond, an experience that would change my life forever.

# The Battle

Crete is the largest of the Greek islands and lies almost 200 miles south of Athens, Greece's capital city. Nowadays, of course, it's a very popular holiday destination. People flock there because it's such a beautiful place. A kind of paradise. But I was there long before the tourists arrived, and during that time, lounging on the beach and soaking up the sun's bright rays wasn't part of the package.

As a consequence of German and Italian attacks, British soldiers had been dispatched to Greece. Crete was important strategically as the Royal Navy defended the eastern Mediterranean. When we arrived there, we thought we were the first members of the British forces to get there, but we were wrong. HMS *Liverpool* had been hit by a torpedo off Crete, and half the rescued crew had been taken to the island.

We were instructed to aim for the far end of Souda Bay, a vast natural harbour which extended over nine miles. From there the chaps from the Navy were to send signals telling us which ships were coming in and at what time.

We were based at an old jail building close to the top end of Souda. I remember that it was all quite strange in a way, because we were quite isolated. When we first got there, we didn't have any vehicles, but in time we were told that a lorry would be available to us. A driver would be needed, therefore, and I was allocated that lofty position. I would run errands here and there, giving us (and me in particular, I suppose) a bit of freedom to move.

We spent a good few weeks with the boys from HMS *Liverpool*, and got on well with them. But, by January 1941, they were instructed to leave the island, to be posted elsewhere. Most of us were very sorry to see them go as we'd established quite a rapport with them. As they left, more troops arrived, however, among them the Welsh Regiment and the Yorks and Lancs, not to mention many, many more. Indeed, by the spring of 1941, there were around 15,000 British troops on the island.

As time went on, we were given more vehicles, and I swapped the heavy lorry for a much lighter vehicle, a motorcycle. There were suspicions that the enemy were picking up some of our signals, so my role was to carry instructions from the Yeoman of Signals down to the bottom end of Souda Bay.

Driven from mainland Greece, British troops had arrived in Crete with very few weapons. Alongside the British on the island, there were also around 7,000 troops from Australia, a similar number from New Zealand and, of course, thousands of Greeks as well. Because so many had arrived unarmed, we had to share some of ours with them.

As tensions in the area increased, the situation well and truly escalated on 20 May, 1941, a date that will always be etched in my memory. This was the day the Germans began to bomb Crete, as part of what was known as Operation Mercury. It became an endless onslaught. For days on end, the bombs rained down. We daren't move. It was safer to stay put as the Messerschmitts circled above us constantly.

The firepower of German planes was undeniably frightening. I can even remember a close encounter with one of their bombs when several of us had been forced to seek refuge in a cave near one of the little beaches. All we heard as we hid was an eerie whistling sound before, a matter of feet away from where we crouched, a bomb landed and sank into the sand. It was within touching distance and we held our breath. Luckily, miraculously even, the bomb didn't explode, and our limbs and lives were spared. But, boy, oh boy, it was an experience that shook me to the core.

That wasn't the last of it. On another day we were digging ditches on a beach when, without any warning, the bombing started again. We had two Irish boys with us, and one of them shouted at me. 'Taff, Taff,' he said. 'Pray! Pray like hell!' As the bombs got nearer and nearer, I really did begin to think that prayer was our only hope of escape. But, yet again, we lived to fight another day.

One evening we were again back on the beach, when we heard a noise. It was dark, and we couldn't see much, but we had a feeling there was something out there in the bay. We contacted the observation post to let them know. We were told not to worry; everything was fine, they said. Less than an hour later the Royal Navy cruiser HMS *York* was hit. Half a dozen or so of small enemy ships had slipped into the bay under the cover of darkness, lethally targeting the *York*. The stricken vessel lay on her side in Souda Bay for years after that, a sad and sobering reminder of the attack.

As fighting continued in late May 1941, many German troops were caught on the beach and taken prisoners. They were brought up to our base in the old jail building by soldiers from the Black Watch, one of whom I had met, as it happens, in Egypt the previous year. I'm not sure which of us was most taken aback at seeing the other again so unexpectedly. Such was the nature of the war experience, however: a series of unfathomable out-of-the-blue events.

That same week one of our ships was hit by a Stuka, one of the German dive bombers. It had been thought that the vessel was in a safe area, but it was clearly not and the ship, and many of her crew, were lost, yet more casualties of an already cruel conflict. During the Battle of Crete, 1,800 naval crew were lost. The German air attacks left their indelible mark on those of us who were land-based, too. Indeed I clearly remember another occasion when we were trying to shelter from aerial bombardment, but this time wearing tin hats. A bomb hit a nearby wall, instantly shattering it. The impact knocked me out; not just me, in fact, but several of us. Lady Luck was on our side, however, and no long-term damage was done. I don't mind admitting, though, it was quite a scare.

One of my fellow soldiers, whose name I forget, had

remarkable intuition, a kind of sixth sense. He would stand on top of a wall and shout, 'They're on their way. I'm telling you they're on their way,' claiming the German bombers would be above us shortly. Initially, we all thought he was spouting nonsense, because we couldn't hear any engine noise at all. Then, within a few seconds, the planes would indeed be above us, and down the bombs would come. I don't know how he did it. He was almost like an Old Testament prophet. Either that or he must have had extraordinary hearing. We soon grew to value his judgement and listen to what he said. I'm convinced his warnings earned us a vital few seconds to try to find shelter from the bombings. In those situations, each and every tiny second could mean the difference between life and death.

Though Crete is the largest of the Greek islands, it's not huge by any means. It's around 160 miles from top to bottom and it's about 35 miles to travel across the island. But from where we were based in the north, it was often difficult to keep up with what was happening elsewhere. I remember on one particular day – it must have been about a week into the battle – we were visited by some of the boys from the RAF who were over there. One of them asked, 'What are you boys doing here?' From his question, we immediately sensed something was wrong. His next question made us realise we were hopelessly out of the loop in terms of being relayed vital information, 'Don't you know that we're evacuating the island?' None of us had heard anything about this; neither had our officers. But this wasn't the time for post-mortems about flaws in the chain of information. It was time to go.

Almost immediately, we made our way south, on foot, over the rugged mountains. We had no maps, and could only gauge our way by aiming for the sun. We walked for hours on end. We couldn't walk much during daylight, however, because the German aeroplanes would be out looking for us. So we trudged along in darkness. By the time we finally made it to the port, it was too late. Our ship had quite literally sailed. We were among a few thousand Allied soldiers who were left behind following the evacuation of many thousands.

Also in Crete at the same time was my neighbour from Dryslwyn, Aneurin Lewis, he whose false teeth we had searched for in vain on an Egyptian beach a year or so earlier! Like me, Aneurin was too late to get on a ship as they evacuated the island. But he was dogged and determined, and no stranger to adventure and peril. He got hold of a small boat and rowed out to sea alone, without any food or water to sustain him. Exposed to the strong sun, and without any shelter, he suffered the effects of sunstroke and dehydration. But, luckily, a British ship spotted him, and he was picked up. It was a case of just in time, apparently, because he was in a bad way, and came very close to dying.

In total, we lost almost 4,000 men during the Battle of Crete. Around 1,800 troops were killed, and a similar number of seamen. It was a bloody and costly battle. A battle we ultimately lost. I think our main problem was a lack of arms. It's not a case of bad workmen blaming the tools because, I'm told, the margins between winning and losing battles can be very thin, and the truth is that without being properly equipped any army will end up being defeated. And that is what happened to us.

Over four nights towards the end of May 1941 some 16,000 Allied troops were shipped safely out of the port of Sfakia. But, another 5,000 or so of us weren't as lucky. A very different fate awaited us.

On 1 June, 1941, we were instructed that we had to surrender or destroy any arms we had. We had been captured by German forces, and were now prisoners of war. An almost deathly silence descended. Escape was not an option. We were surrounded by armed German soldiers. Days after making the journey down from the north of the island, we were told that we would be walking every step of the way back up again. To say that our morale was low was an understatement. Many of us felt broken. But we would have to find a will and a way from somewhere to keep our spirits up. Although we were captured, we had to make sure that we weren't mentally defeated. As bodies weakened, more than ever, strong minds were required now.

We'd probably gone the best part of two weeks eating very little. It was getting hotter every day, and we were dehydrated. We were living on very limited rations. I remember there was a hard biscuit, which almost broke your teeth when you bit into it. It looked, and probably tasted, like a dog biscuit. We were also given the odd tin of corned beef to share between ten of us or so. The old saying is, of course, that an army marches on its stomach. If that is the case, I really don't know how we managed to make it back up to the north of the island on so little food.

I remember passing through one village where a little old lady came out and offered us some olives. If I'm honest, those olives weren't much to my liking. But, it was a gesture of extreme kindness, which angered the German soldiers. I think little things like that – the generosity and support shown by local people – helped to lift our spirits. After three days of hard walking, we made it back up to the north, and arrived at Maleme, where the old aerodrome would become our prison.

We weren't surrounded by big walls or tall barbed wire fences at Maleme. Everything was quite open. But, in truth, because most of us felt so physically weak and mentally drained, due to a lack of food and general exhaustion, any thoughts of escape were well and truly cast aside. Many of us had dysentery and terrible diarrhoea. We'd go to the medics at the camp, but they didn't have anything to give us, really. The stock answer was usually, 'We've only got soda bic [sodium bicarbonate], nothing else.' It was pitiful.

I suffered badly with dysentery. I was as thin as a rake. My legs felt hollow and weak, and I really thought I was going to die. But, somehow, over time I gradually recovered. Someone must have been watching over me.

I remember one day a German soldier asked a group of us if any of us could pluck a chicken which they had caught and killed. Immediately, I said I could. I did the job, and my reward was a small tin of meat. Well, the little tin seemed like a great feast, and I think it helped to give me some strength. It's strange how little things can make a big difference in difficult times.

When I felt stronger, I came across another fellow prisoner who'd had enough of being kept under German rule. 'I feel sick of this place, and I've got to get out,' he said. For the first time since we'd been incarcerated, escape was on the agenda.

The road towards Maleme itself lay opposite the aerodrome-cum-prison. Because it was such an open location, making our exit was a relatively straightforward process, or that's we thought, at least. We both watched patiently as a handful of guards ambled back and forth. Then, as they walked away in another direction, we seized our chance and made a run for it. And we got away.

We must have been gone for a couple of days when the young soldier who was with me fell ill. The stifling heat and lack of food and water meant that he deteriorated quickly. He whispered that he thought he was dying. I had no option but to try to get him back to the aerodrome. The escape attempt had to be aborted. But, ironically, trying to make our way back proved far more problematic than escaping in the first place, because I had to physically drag and carry my colleague back. And in the searing conditions, it was nothing short of gruelling.

After what seemed like days of punishing physical effort, we neared the aerodrome. I saw the German guards on parade, and decided it was best to make our way towards them, and to face any consequences. To be honest, I was too exhausted to worry too much about those. As it happens, the guards did not recognise us: they thought we were two British soldiers surrendering ourselves. We were sent down to see the medics, where I was instructed to leave my stricken colleague with them. I don't know what happened to him. I never saw him again.

If the escape experience had sapped my energy, it definitely hadn't dampened my spirit to try to flee the enemy's grasp. After a few days' rest, I left the aerodrome again. This time, on my own. I walked for more than a day, concentrating on keeping away from villages and people. But, the quest for water and food got the better of me. I could see a collection of houses in the distance, and made my way towards them. I called at one of the first places I saw. It was a very modest place, but the people who lived there were welcoming. They probably didn't have much themselves but they gave me something to eat and drink, without any trouble at all. They realised I was a British soldier, and they knew I was on the run.

I decided to take stock, and stay within the confines of the village for a day or two, just to get stronger. But, I soon realised that there was tension locally, and that some in the village weren't too keen to have me there. I can't blame them. They knew that anyone found helping or harbouring an escaped prisoner of war would face serious recriminations from the Nazi forces on the island. One local man had enough English to tell me that it would be best for me to move on. I didn't want to put anyone's life in danger, and I heeded the advice. I don't know exactly how far I'd got from the aerodrome, but I'm guessing it must have been 20 miles or so. But, in truth, I didn't really see how I was going to stay at large for any length of time. And where was I going to go, anyway? I decided that the best thing to do was to return. So, once again, I trudged my way back to the aerodrome.

Not long after, prisoners were given an opportunity to go out to work, under the supervision of the German guards, of course. As well as providing a break from the monotony of prison life, going out to work came with a promise of food as well. There was very little of that on offer at the aerodrome, so I volunteered to go out on the labour lorries. They took us out every day, about 15 of us, and we had to work hard for our food.

It was difficult and depressing work. Victory in the Battle of Crete had come at a heavy human cost for the Germans, too. About 4,000 of their men had been killed, and their bodies needed to be buried. And that was the grisly task that lay ahead. The heap of bodies had been there for days. It was hot. They had swollen up, and the stench was terrible. We dug the graves. As well as the mental challenge, it was also physically demanding. The soil was very different to the rich, yielding farmland of the Tywi valley in Carmarthenshire. It was like digging into a rock.

One morning I was a few minutes late for work: the labour lorry was already pulling away, so I tried to jump on. Then one of the German guards intervened, kicking me until my legs gave way, and I fell to the floor. In fairness, one of the German officers witnessed the incident, and he tore a strip off the guard there and then. The officer then turned to me and told me to come back tomorrow, assuring me that there would be a place for me on the lorry. He was as good as his word. But some of the German guards were often heavy-handed. It was the way things were, and we had to get used to it. We were in the middle of a war, and normal codes of behaviour no longer applied.

Several of the boys in my working party were from New Zealand and Australia. One day, one of them was seen carrying the body of a local man who had been caught up in the fighting. He had brought it over for burial, but on seeing the body a German guard responded angrily: 'Get *that* out of here!'

'We don't bury dogs,' he said. We couldn't believe how cruel he was. One of the Aussies just couldn't hold back. 'Look,' he shouted. 'If he's a dog, you're a bloody rat!'

Uproar ensued. The German guard took out his gun and fired a shot into the air. We all scattered, and half a dozen German soldiers scurried over to see what the commotion was. A German officer asked the guard who exactly had called him a 'bloody rat'. His response was immediate: 'Blond'. But as the German officer looked around, there wasn't a blond-haired soldier in sight. The Aussie must have scarpered when the gun was fired. Luckily, things calmed down and the tension was diffused. But we weren't allowed to bury the local man's body.

At the time, not far from Maleme, on the way to Chania,

the Germans were erecting some kind of statue with the Nazi eagle on top. We had been ordered to go there, to help mix cement and to lend a hand with the building work. One of the British soldiers over there was called Moc Morgan, a big, strong chap who was a member of the Welch Regiment. Many of the Germans prided themselves on their strength, and maintained they were far stronger than us. But they met their match in Moc Morgan. I remember him lifting two sacks of cement and putting them under each arm and then walking with them. The Germans then tried to copy him – and failed miserably. He was something else. A real natural strongman. And even the Germans had to admit defeat.

We were probably among the last group of soldiers to leave Crete. When we were instructed to make our way down to Souda Bay, we knew that our time on the island was coming to an end. We were told to board an overcrowded vessel, and in cramped, oppressive conditions we headed for Salonika on the Greek mainland.

When we arrived, we were marched through a nearby town where I remember a gang of local boys, some as young as ten, giving us bread. A little old lady also came to meet us with bread that she'd cut up for us. But the Germans didn't like these acts of local kindness one bit, so much so that one of them struck the old lady in the face with his gun, until there was blood everywhere. As unnecessary as it was cruel, it was an act which shocked and angered us in equal measure. If we hadn't been so heavily outnumbered, I'm sure we would have taken the Germans on there and then.

On we went to our destination: an old barracks a few miles from Salonika, where there was neither food nor water. After three or four days there, we were escorted to the nearest railway station. There we were put in containers, the kind normally used to transport animals, cattle in all probability. There was no room to lie down or even to sit. There was no light, either. It was cripplingly uncomfortable. What is more, we didn't know where we were going or what our fate would be. It was a journey, quite literally, into the dark. But I clung on to the one cause which I had for hope – I was still alive.

# Behind the Wire

Every now and then the train would stop, probably to stock up on coal. On those occasions the door would open and a guard would come in with a bucket of water. That might sound a lot of water, but that single bucket had to be shared between all of us. We were about 40 in total, crammed together like sardines, so it was nothing, really. The container reeked of the worst kind of human odour, and I remember feeling that I was forever fighting the urge to vomit. The only thing which stopped me was that I had next to nothing in my stomach to throw up. I don't know how we got through it. But, after three long days, we reached a place called Wolfsberg, in southern Austria.

As we stumbled out of the station, we immediately sensed a hostile atmosphere. We were not welcome here. People lined both sides of the road, and even the little children were shouting at us. It was heartbreaking to witness. Since 1938 Austria had, of course, been under Nazi rule, and during the war around a million Austrians served in the German army. And, it was obvious that the Nazi grip on Wolfsberg was a crushing one.

What lay before us was the camp. Even from outside, Stalag 18A seemed an intimidating place. It was the archetypal prisoner of war camp. A tall perimeter fence ran around the outer limits, rimmed with ominous curls of barbed wire. Inside there were more fences and little wooden huts. Armed German guards patrolled the avenues between the huts, some exuding authority, others sheer menace. Hundreds of POWs were incarcerated here. And they weren't just British. There were Australians, New Zealanders and French soldiers. Not long afterwards, scores of Russians arrived as well.

There were several watchtowers dotted around the camp, to monitor every move. From our very first day at the Stalag, therefore, we knew that this was a million miles away from the makeshift prison camp at the aerodrome in Crete. This was the real thing, and the message was simple, but chilling: 'Try to escape from here, and you will be shot.'

By the time we had arrived, many of the other prisoners had already been there for several weeks, if not months. From them we learnt that every prisoner was given a tin on arrival, and everything we had in terms of food was to be consumed out of that tin. We had to queue and wait to be fed in turn. The food was totally unappetising, and there was very little of it. I remember there was some kind of very weak and bland potato soup. But, it was better than nothing.

Within a few weeks parcels arrived from the Red Cross, and these were a godsend. They included tea bags, chocolate, cigarettes and little things like that, but they were all lifesavers. I didn't smoke, personally, but I could still use the cigarettes as currency, swapping them for some extra tea bags or a little bar of chocolate.

No one expects prison to be a pleasant environment, especially in wartime, but there was an atmosphere at Stalag 18A which I despised from day one. There was, however, one element which provided a glimmer of hope. Stalag 18A was known in German as an *arbeitskommando*, a work camp. POWs were given hard labour tasks and very often this meant going out to work in gangs in factories, farms, and other workplaces, under Nazi supervision. In truth, I didn't mind that at all. Since my childhood and the dark days of the Depression in the 1930s, mine had always been a robust work ethic. It was engrained in me.

Very soon I found myself in a place called Knittelfeld, a small town on the banks of the river Mur, about 40 miles north of Wolfsberg and Stalag 18A. There was quite a large brickworks in Knittelfeld, and a gang of us were sent to work there. Between 15 and 20 of us stayed in a house nearby, a house belonging to the owner of the brickworks, and we slept in bunk beds. At seven o'clock sharp every morning we started our shift. It was physical work, often cutting clay, and loading it into trucks. Then there'd be days when we'd shape the bricks to be placed in the kiln. And then we'd have to load the kiln with enough coal to maintain its heat.

Without doubt, the hardest job was digging the clay out of the ground. It was as if we were hitting concrete. It really was back-breaking. The brickwork owner was Italian. A large man with a huge stomach, he very often berated us for not working quickly or hard enough. On one such occasion when he was particularly critical, one of our boys snapped. He turned to the brickwork owner and said, 'Listen, if we were given even half the food you so very obviously eat, we'd have a lot more energy and could work so much harder!' He didn't like hearing that at all, but there was a lot of truth in it.

After a while, we managed to get hold of some potatoes which were growing nearby. Having strung them on a piece of wire, they were then placed in the brick kilns, and such was the heat of those makeshift ovens that the spuds were baked in no time. Perfect jacket potatoes! And they were delicious.

Whilst I was in Knittelfeld, I was laid low by malaria again: it's a disease that doesn't go away easily, unfortunately. Suddenly I was weak and housebound, and temporarily given kitchen duties. Whilst I was working there, I started talking with the daughter of the owner of the brickworks. She was friendly and had good English. Apparently, she'd spent some time working as a nanny at the German Embassy in London before the war. She gave me an English book to read when I was ill. I forget the title of the book, or what it was about even, but I do remember her kindness.

Every Friday evening we were allowed to walk into the town of Knittelfeld itself. There was a large steelworks in the town, and there were showers there where the workers would go to wash at the end of a hard day's shift. Every Friday, we could go there to have a shower. As a rule, we washed our clothes at the same time. On the way back, the guards who'd accompany us would allow us to have one quick drink in a local alehouse. We were strongly instructed not to tell anyone in authority about the Friday night drink, and, of course, that was one little secret we were all quite willing to keep.

In time we were moved on from Knittelfeld to work in another town about 40 miles west, a place called Murau, where we initially worked on a building site. We slept in an old stable block near the bridge spanning the river Mur which flowed through the centre of the town.

When we arrived at our sleeping quarters, there were met by a deputation from the German army, along with a local man, who had very good English. I think he was the Mayor of Murau, and he was certainly quite welcoming. As he addressed us, however, we could hear one of the German officers muttering something in the background. One of our boys asked the English-speaking official what had just been said. His answer was brief, but sobering. 'He's just saying that if you try to escape from here, you will be shot.'

As the officer who had issued that threat left, one of our gang shouted, 'I hope you drop dead, you old bugger!' Thankfully, I don't think the officer understood what the POW said, but the sequel to this episode was unbelievable. We heard the next day that that same German officer had indeed collapsed and died! We had only met him briefly, of course, and in less than favourable circumstances, but the news of his death still sent a chill down the spine.

Despite its being wartime, when tensions naturally ran high, not one of us POWs truly wanted the officer dead. As we reflected on the news, an eerie silence fell.

I also have warmer memories of Murau, particularly of the local butcher who regularly fed us. Very often, I was the one entrusted with the task of collecting those supplies from his shop in the evening. Whilst I waited for the food to be prepared, I often got talking to locals and gradually I started to pick up some basic German. Over time my vocabulary improved, so I came to understand more and became more confident in speaking the language. The butcher and his family were very kind towards us, and gave us as much food as they could.

After a few weeks on the building site in Murau, some of us were given the opportunity to work at the hydroelectric station on the outskirts of the town. Three of us volunteered straightaway: Dougie Arthur from Liverpool (I'm still in contact with him), Geoff Hallett from Cardiff, and me. Our responsibility was to ensure that the water which flowed to the turbines was clean. We used big rakes to take out any stones or small branches. The work was much harder than it sounds, and the Austrian winters were very cold. I remember one painful occasion when Geoff's hands froze and literally stuck to the rake. After that, we all made sure that we'd wrap a piece of cloth around our hands as a protective layer before handling the rake.

In the depths of winter it was common to see ice a foot deep paralysing the river. That meant that there was very little water making its way down the valley. So, Herr

Moshammer, who supervised our work at the hydroelectric station, would have to make little holes in the ice and put dynamite in them to shatter it. The water would then start to flow, and it was business as usual. A local man with no connection to the German authorities, Franz Moshammer was a very pleasant chap, who treated us with kindness and respect.

Very often we would give some of the chocolate from our Red Cross parcels to Moshammer, as a little gift for his children. And we would often get some food in return from the Austrian and his family. The respect between us was mutual, therefore. On one occasion he even tried to teach us to ski. It was a lot of fun, but I think he realised very soon he wasn't going to turn us into world champions on the piste.

The manager of the hydroelectric station was Herr Ferdinand Zeiper. He must have been in his thirties at the time. He too was very fair in his dealings with us. He quite rightly expected us to work hard, but he never exploited us. He made sure we had regular breaks. I remember him as a quiet man, but he had an air of strength and authority about him at the same time. But most of all there was a respect there, which again went both ways.

We also got to know some of the locals outside work. Indeed, one of them asked me one day if I'd ever killed a pig! When I said that I had, he invited me to his house. There, I helped him catch his pig, before it was hung upside down and its throat was slit. He was well prepared, because he had a container in place to catch the blood which streamed from the pig's body. A few days after that, the Austrian said he wanted to give me a present for helping him kill the pig. It was *blutwurst*, a speciality sausage made of pork and blood. I'd never tried it before, but I was pleasantly surprised. It was very tasty!

I often wondered what would have happened to that man had the German officers found out that he had befriended a POW. I'm sure he would have found himself the victim of unpleasant retribution. In those strange times we came across people who showed kindness towards us. They were simple gestures from ordinary people. They weren't part of any army. And their attitude made our lives that little bit easier.

# Hard Labour

The next port of call was Stadl an der Mur, about ten miles from Murau, and the task ahead of us here was very different. We would be working in the forest, and based at a hunting lodge nearby. But the hospitality of our German army hosts didn't stretch to allowing us to be accommodated in the lodge itself. We had no delusions of grandeur. We knew our place, and that was firmly in the lodge's stables.

We slept in bunks. They weren't the most comfortable, but we had a roof over our heads. Even in the depths of winter, the work kept us warm. Again, it was physical stuff. We learned how to chop down big trees the proper way, and how to cut the wood and treat it as well. We were all quite able lumberjacks within a few weeks. We would saw the wood into three-yard pieces, and sharpen the point of each one. We'd then place piles of wood on the frozen river in such a way that when the frost melted, the wood would be carried neatly down the river by the current. When it reached the valley floor, it would be sorted, ready for distribution.

There were several areas in the forest surrounded by high fences, and we soon found out that these were deer enclosures. I remember one day I caught a young deer, and hoped that we could slaughter it, thus providing us with a meaty source of much needed winter nourishment. But our supervisor didn't approve at all: the deer was given a stay of execution, and released to fight another day.

Whilst we were in Stadl, one of our boys was taken severely ill. His name was Ken and he had an extremely high temperature. As luck would have it, however, one of the people who passed through the forest on horseback that day was in fact a doctor. He was getting on a bit, but he was calm and assured. He examined Ken, before telling us to wrap a blanket around him and carry him out to the river. It was a really cold day and the river was frozen in parts, so what came next surprised us. He told us to place the patient in the water! We shuddered. The cold water would kill him, wouldn't it? But, the old medic assured us that the freezing water would actually help Ken. So in he was dipped for a few seconds which must have felt an age for poor Ken. We then lifted him out, took him back to the stable, and dried him off, before placing him back in the bed, still not convinced that this would aid his recovery in any way. But, lo and behold, within a few days, Ken was back to his old self. How he'd been cured, I'm still not sure? Maybe that icy stretch of water had, in fact, been holy water!

The area where we worked was surrounded by a high wire fence, so the chances of escape were minimal. One day, a guard sent me to fetch some charcoal from a local man who made it nearby. We got talking but found communication difficult, since a combination of his pronounced local dialect and my broken German meant that neither of us of really understood what the other was saying! The result of our discourse was that he disappeared into his shed before re-emerging a few seconds later with a little bottle. If I understood correctly, the bottle contained the liquid which seeped out of the wood during the charcoal-making process, and he urged me to try some, which I did. What a hit! The roof of my mouth was on fire, and my eyes were watering. This was seriously strong stuff.

'Take a bottle with you,' he insisted. That night, back in the stable, I showed my room-mates what I'd been given. Everyone was up for a tasting session. But no one took a second swig! It was the strongest thing any of us had tasted. I can honestly say that I've never drunk anything else before or since which has come close to it, thank God!

There was one expansive open hillside space in Stadl an der Mur and, as I was crossing it one winter's day, a childhood memory came flooding back. I remembered how, when the snow and ice had descended in our Carmarthenshire village, we'd each get hold of a flat piece of wood, and slide down the hill as fast as we could on our improvised sledges. It was a source of much merriment. So, I decided to try to replicate that feeling on the Austrian slopes. When the other boys saw me doing this, they joined in as well. We laughed like children as we raced down the slope, slipping and sliding as we went. The fun didn't last long, of course, but at least it was some respite from hard labour and Nazi rule.

Hard work was both our punishment and salvation, but it was also monotonous. And what I hated more than anything was that we weren't free. Despite the fact that we got our fair share of fresh air and no little exercise, we were prisoners of war. I longed for freedom. Very soon my thoughts turned again towards planning an escape.

I was contemplating making my way through the forest, walking over the mountains and across the border to Switzerland. Indeed whilst we were out working one day I even asked a local forester how far it was to Switzerland. He was obviously taken aback by my question. 'My dear fellow,' he said. 'You would never be able to walk to Switzerland from here. You would get lost in the forest in no time. It would just be an impossible task.'

Hearing that was such a blow, because it came from a man who truly knew the lie of the land. He knew the forest and the area well, and if he said it would be impossible to get away, then I had to accept that he was right. But I was still left thinking that there must be another way out, another means of escape.

One thing I definitely couldn't escape from was malaria. As is the nature of the illness, it kept on coming back. A bad penny if ever there was one. There were times when I had to stay in our stables for days on end to try to get over a bout. I remember one occasion in particular when I was left on my own, after all the guards had gone to supervise my colleagues in the forest. I took advantage of the peace and quiet to have a good look around the place. Above the stables was a loft. I went up there to have a peek. I found a little bolthole up there, where I was sure I could make my way out one night, without the guards seeing me.

But my plans came to nothing when we were told one morning to get our things together. We would be leaving Stadl an der Mur. We would be heading for Tamsweg, about 12 miles away. Several of the boys were looking forward to a change of scene. I couldn't help thinking to myself that I'd just missed my big opportunity to escape.

Once we got to Tamsweg we could see that our *lager* – German for 'camp' – had been especially prepared for us. It had a high wire fence all the way around, to deter anyone with thoughts of escape. We arrived there in summer, in time for haymaking, which was work I was used to, having helped out on several farms in Carmarthenshire. For my fellow POWs, however, this was a new experience in an alien environment. But, to be fair to them, within a few days even the city boys of Liverpool and Cardiff among them had become quite adept at handling a scythe. I was impressed. 'Boys, we'll make farmers out of you yet,' I said.

Tamsweg was very rural and I jumped at the chance to work outside in the summer. The hills were full of blueberries, I recall, and when I started to collect them, my city friends had no idea what they were. They'd never seen them before. When I said they were edible, most of them pulled a face, and one or two even thought they were poisonous. My fellow Welshman, Geoff Hallett, and I thought it would be a good idea to make some kind of stew with the blueberries. Of course, we didn't have any proper ingredients to cook with. We didn't even have sugar, and I remember when we served up our speciality dish, the taste was very sour, to say the least.

'Take that bloody thing out and don't make it again,' was how one of the boys responded. But some began to acquire a taste for blueberries, even if they were in their raw, rather than cooked form. It's surprising what people will eat when food is scarce.

In Tamsweg, we were joined by a handful of New Zealanders, one of whom was a proficient barber. His arrival was particularly welcomed, given the unkempt state of our hair after the difficulties and exertions of the last few months. In time I got chatting with him and he asked me from where I came. I stuck my chest out and stated proudly, 'Wales!'

'Funny you should say that, mate,' said the barber. 'We had a Welshman working with us in the mine.' Apparently, before they had arrived in Tamsweg, the New Zealanders had been working in a coal mine in another part of Austria.

'This Welsh guy could really sing,' said the barber. I told him that this was true of many Welshmen, even if I wasn't much of a singer myself, and in the name of polite conversation (and curiosity) I pressed him further about the sonorous Welsh miner: 'Do you remember his name?' And he did.

'Enoch. Wally Enoch.'

'Good God,' I exclaimed. 'Wally Enoch lives less than five miles from me back home!'

Wally lived in a village called Pontargothi, and was well

known in our area as a very accomplished exponent of the modern songs which were popular at the time. But, even so, it was quite a shock to hear about his musical exploits from a New Zealander in rural Austria.

Another of the Kiwis, as we called the boys from New Zealand, was quite a character. He was a forester back home before the war, and I remember the day he held up one of his hands to show us that he had lost three of his fingers. 'How did that happen?' I asked.

'We've got this game in New Zealand,' he said. 'You lay your hand out flat on a piece of wood. You spread your fingers out as widely as you can. And then someone comes with an axe and, without pausing, goes bang, bang, bang, bang, between each of your fingers.'

'Well, he certainly got you, didn't he?' I said.

'Oh, no, mate. That was my fault,' said the Kiwi, with a wry smile on his face. 'I lost my nerve and moved my hand.'

He'd said he'd show me how it was done.

'No, thanks,' I said, without even half a second's hesitation. 'I'd quite like to hang on to all my fingers, thank you,' I told him.

'No, I don't mean using your hand,' said the Kiwi. 'There's another way.'

He drew an outline of a hand on a piece of wood, and then grabbed an axe. Down it came four times in rapid succession, expertly landing between each of the fingers on the outline in turn. He did so without touching any of the fingers he'd drawn. He was quite a craftsman, evidently. But, for all his skill, I was still very relieved that he was using a piece of wood rather than my hand for his demonstration.

At short notice, and after only a very brief stay, we were told that we were on the move again. We would be leaving Tamsweg for Kaltwasser, back near Stadl an der Mur. There we came across a very formidable woman working in the kitchen. I hope I'm not being unkind when I say that she was quite masculine in both appearance and behaviour. What is more, she wasn't to be crossed. Indeed, such was her threatening demeanour that some of the boys referred to her as 'the old cow'.

One day she asked me in German, 'Tell me what does this word "oldcow" mean?' What was I supposed to say? She had caught me off guard, so I tried to buy thinking time, knowing that I had to tread with extreme caution. She must have sensed my unease before I eventually spluttered out, 'Oh, if you think a lot of somebody and you hold them in very high esteem, you refer to them an "old cow".'

It did not sound convincing. Incredibly, however, she seemed to accept my translation.

A week later the same woman made a beeline towards me. I could see by the look on her face that she was not happy, more so than usual. 'Oldcow, oldcow,' she shouted. 'I know what it means,' almost screaming. I swallowed hard. The game was up. But I thought I'd have one more stab at preserving her dignity and saving my own skin into the bargain.

'Listen now,' I said. 'Like me, you are from a rural

background. And back home, when we come across somebody who is a nice, down-to-earth person we often call them an "old cow". It's a term of endearment.'

Miraculously, she calmed down. She had bought my explanation – and I had managed to get out of what had seemed an ever deepening hole. What a relief!

At Kaltwasser we were subjected to regular inspections. The officer in charge of these learnt that I spoke some German so I was instructed to translate his pronouncements to the POWs. This proved a tall order. The officer spoke quickly, and in quite academic German, certainly not the colloquial variety to which I'd grown accustomed. I found myself making it up as I went along, and one of the boys realised my predicament and started laughing.

Unfortunately, the officer didn't see the funny side of things. He grew red in the face and started shouting. To say he was angry would be an understatement. He reached for his gun and pulled it out. The sergeant saw this and screamed, 'No, no.' I turned to the officer and said, 'He was laughing at me, sir. At me, not you!' Luckily the German officer was pacified. But I'm convinced the New Zealander who laughed out loud came within a whisker of being shot there and then.

I had other concerns about language, too, but not about German or English. During all this time I had heard no Welsh spoken at all. Welsh was my mother tongue, my first language, and I started to fret that I might be losing it because I wasn't getting a chance to hear it, let alone speak it. So, I deliberately set to thinking back to my school days, as I tried to recall the Welsh poems I had learnt during that time. Gradually, lines written by poets such as Ceiriog and Eifion Wyn came back, reformed through the mists of time. Likewise I reached for those verses I learned at Sunday School, especially Psalm 23, and I would start reciting 'Yr Arglwydd yw fy mugail...' ('The Lord is my shepherd...') and so on out loud. The other POWs would laugh when they heard me at it. 'Taff,' they'd say. 'You're talking to yourself again.'

But, I'm convinced it was a strategy that worked for me. It kept the language alive in my mind and on my lips, and it was an important connection with home and stability at such an uncertain time.

After a few weeks in Kaltwasser, we upped sticks yet again, this time to Sankt Lambrecht, about 20 miles to the east. We were held in an old monastery, a striking, imposing place built for the Benedictine order in the 11th century. By the time we got to Sankt Lambrecht the monks had long departed, and the Nazis ruled the roost there. Despite the monastery's beauty and serenity, we were kept in a cold uncomfortable block.

But I didn't stay there for long. The malaria had returned and I was so weak that it was decided I wasn't well enough to stay there and work in the potato fields with the other POWs. There was no alternative: I was going back to Wolfsberg, and Stalag 18A.

# Back to the Stalag

There was a stench around Stalag 18A. I don't know exactly what it was. But it was there all the time; you couldn't get away from it. I'd been away from the Stalag for a year or more, at different work camps around Austria. And on the whole, we'd been treated quite well, or at least as well as you could expect to be treated as a prisoner of war. Yes, the work had been hard and the hours long, but we did get some fresh air and exercise, despite being under Nazi rule. At the Stalag, life was very different.

Stalag is the short form of *Stammlager*, the German term for a prisoner of war camp for non-commissioned personnel, or quite simply soldiers who aren't officers. Every prisoner was given an individual number. I remember mine to this day: 5382.

I'd left the unyielding surroundings of the prisoner block at Sankt Lambrecht monastery, and Stalag 18A hardly offered any more in terms of comfort. Indeed, it was a most forbidding place. We slept in rows of bunks in wooden huts. The beds were hard and lumpy – the makeshift mattresses were little better than sacks filled with straw. Everyone had a blanket each. The food was poor and there was very little of it. There very few washing facilities and toilets, either. But, compared to some of the other inmates, we – the 200 or so British soldiers who were there at the same time as me – lived a pretty charmed life.

I arrived back at the Stalag in the winter of 1942, by which time there were hundreds of Russian prisoners there. Russia wasn't part of the Geneva Convention, and consequently their prisoners weren't eligible for the Red Cross parcels distributed to other inmates. Whereas we could look forward to the odd bar of chocolate or a tin of meat or fish, the Russians had nothing except those few scraps they were given at the camp.

In truth, the Nazis were incredibly cruel towards them, treating them like animals. It really was shocking. They were kept apart from all the other prisoners, fenced off in their own compound. They looked terrible and I really felt for them: they were skin and bone, and no more. Some were dressed in rags; some had no clothes at all, only a blanket wrapped around them. Many of them had nothing on their feet.

We would come face to face with them at the fence which was always between us, and throw them a few scraps of food if we could, pieces of bread or whatever we could lay our hands on. We weren't supposed to do that, of course, and the Germans would try to stop us. But we just wanted to show some compassion, a literal crumb of kindness.

The saddest thing of all to witness, however, was what sometimes happened when we threw the food over the fence. Mayhem ensued as the starving Russians summoned up what little energy they could from their weak bodies to grapple with each other for the scraps that came their way. It was a heartbreaking sight. I really couldn't believe what I was seeing. Had humanity really come to this?

Many of the Russians were seriously ill, many the victims of typhus, an infectious disease which thrives among the malnourished in dirty conditions where there is very little clean water. Tens of them died every day. There were scores of burials several times a week. We watched and felt utterly useless. There was nothing at all we could to do to assist these poor people, or alleviate their suffering in any way.

And, though we didn't know it at the time, there were very sinister things going on at Stalag 18A. It seems that the Nazis were conducting a programme of research experiments on some of the prisoners. It later became apparent that Nazi scientists had been measuring the heads of hundreds of prisoners from different nations, and making casts of their faces. The aim, it appears, was to prove the supremacy as the German 'master race'. As we had certain rights under international law, the British, thankfully, refused to take part in these sickening experiments.

For me, the Nazis humiliated individual men and diminished mankind by experimenting on defenceless POWs. When someone has descended to that level, they have reached the very bottom of human depravity. I was brought up to believe that all people are equal, whatever their nationality, creed or colour. And these experiments were the antithesis of all this. But, of course, it was the deluded belief that his nation, his people, were better than any other on earth that drove Hitler, and that was what made him such a dangerous and evil man.

I've no doubt that some truly horrendous things happened behind the barbed wire of Stalag 18A. And despite how tough life was, we had to try and put these horrors out of our mind. That was the only way to survive. All I tried to do was focus on survival. Just survival. If I had contemplated too deeply all that was happening and might happen, I would have found it impossible to concentrate fully on what needed to be done. And for me, there was one thing I wanted to do more than anything else, and that was to escape. To escape to freedom.

# The Big Chance

The spring months of 1943 brought some much needed relief from the harsh Austrian winter. It was also a time when an opportunity arose to leave the oppressive regime and bleak surroundings of the Stalag. By early summer I was one of a group of POWs who had been posted to Gaas in north eastern Austria, close to the border with Hungary. The task ahead of us was farm labour. That suited me, and about ten of us made the 100-mile journey from Wolfsberg.

Gaas was a quiet village in an area where agriculture was the mainstay, just as it was in rural Carmarthenshire. Because so many men had been conscripted to the German army, there was a serious shortage of agricultural labour. POWs like us filled that gap. All day, every day, we would work in the fields. In the evenings we would then be shepherded back to the *lager* – the camp where we were held on the outskirts of the village.

Straightaway we sensed that life was going to be significantly better than it was in the Stalag. There was the chance to work outdoors, and enjoy the beautiful countryside, of course. But, more than that, there was the promise of being fed on the farms, in return for our labour.

And this was home-cooked fresh food, not the bland or often rotten fodder we were given at the Stalag.

I worked on a farm belonging to an elderly woman called Agnes Kraller. From the beginning she showed me kindness and respect. She was friendly and fair. There was a younger woman at the farm as well, whose husband was away in the German army. I'm not sure where he was stationed or what he was doing, but his young wife wasn't as friendly as Agnes. Who knows that she didn't resent us because we were the enemy, her husband's enemy? And if she chose to be distant, who could blame her?

Next door to the farm was a vineyard. One day I was out there helping Agnes, picking grapes and generally pottering around. There must have been about a dozen other women helping out that day as well, so it was all hustle and bustle. But then, above the chatter, we heard a piercing scream. Suddenly we saw some of the women running towards the noise. I followed them, but I was told to stand back: this was no place for a man, apparently. The source of the scream was one of the younger women working in the vineyard: she had just given birth!

It wasn't long before the young woman emerged with her baby safely clutched in her arms, in a makeshift wrap. It had all happened so quickly, but she looked in rude health. It was good to know that the scream had given way to a happy ending. It had been no ordinary day, and I had an interesting story to tell the other POWs at the *lager* that night.

A week or two later I was out ploughing in the fields.

The plough was drawn by two strong bullocks and led by a young boy who was perched on top of one of them, which was quite a common sight in that corner of Austria. It was my job to steer the plough from behind, making sure the furrow was as straight as possible. Whilst this required a good deal of concentration, it wasn't physically demanding because the soil was soft and lush.

The area we were ploughing was vast and flat, and broken into distinct, clearly-marked sections, each belonging to a different farmer. Another POW worked nearby, ploughing with two big horses. I tried to establish eye contact, but he kept his head down, and didn't look around much. One day, however, I saw him pacing an area of the field, without his horses. I soon realised that he was measuring the land, from the field we were ploughing to the bridge which crossed the Pinka river nearby. The Pinka marked the natural border between Austria and Hungary.

A few evenings later I saw the POW again, and decided to go over and introduce myself. He was polite enough, but didn't seem too keen to engage in conversation. His name was Roy Natusch. He was tall and strong, with dark hair and a moustache, and had the look of a film star about him. He was from New Zealand, a skilful rugby player it transpired, who had been an All Black trialist no less before the war. But he didn't give much away.

'I could see you measuring the land a few days ago,' I told him. He looked at me intently for a few seconds, before responding brusquely, 'What is it to you? It's no business of yours.'

We hadn't got off to the best of starts, but I wasn't going to give up.

'Well, I thought that you and I may have been thinking along the same lines,' I said.

'Oh. And what lines are those?' was his curt reply.

I then explained that I was keen to attempt an escape across the border to Hungary, and on to freedom. He saw I was serious, and there was a spark in his eye. He paused for a second or two, and then said, 'Well, mate, I think we may well be thinking the same way. Let's talk some more.'

From that moment on, there was a bond between us. We shook hands and began to hatch our plans. Escape had suddenly become so much more than a dream.

On foot our camp was a good hour-and-a-half from the border. And, of course, there were soldiers guarding the crossing point. On the Austrian side, the Nazis kept a close watch, whilst the other side was patrolled by Hungarian troops. Escape, therefore, meant not only successfully negotiating one checkpoint, but two. We were under no illusions. We knew we were facing a difficult task. But, we were both very determined souls, who weren't going to be easily deterred. With careful planning, we firmly believed we could make it to Hungary safely. But we knew that failure would bring with it very grave consequences.

Over the next few days and weeks we did more measuring work. We mapped out the area in detailed and methodical fashion, coming to the conclusion that our best chance of escape was to follow a route that went *between* the two checkpoints. It was agreed that those plans were to be a sworn secret. We would tell no one. The more people who knew, the more exposed we would be.

On the farm where Roy worked were loads of onions, and he started bringing a few back to the camp. We chopped them up, threw them into a large bucket, and poured water over them. We then hid the bucket in a storeroom at the back of the *lager*. There was a method to all this madness, which I'll come to shortly.

Roy also noticed a little nook in the storeroom where we could hide some more supplies which would be useful if and when we escaped. Gradually an enviable stash built up containing bars of chocolate, some tins of meat, fish and condensed milk. After all, we might be on the run for quite a while before we reached a safe place in Hungary, so these supplies would help keep our strength up as winter took hold.

By early December 1943 there was no sign of the heavy snow that usually engulfed Austria at that time of year. Indeed it was quite mild. We decided that the time was right to make a run for it.

Roy and I had been quite circumspect and had managed to keep our plans to ourselves. But one day, one of our boys overheard one of our conversations, and worked out that we were thinking of escaping. He was Len Caulfield, an Englishman, and naturally he wanted to come with us. The plot thickened, however. Len told another POW – Joe Walker from County Durham – about our plans, so he, too, wanted to come. Joe was a very small, slight man, and we were worried whether he truly realised how tough any escape was likely to be. We felt also that four people would be too many: it would increase our risk of being spotted and caught. So, we had to tell Joe that we just couldn't let him come with us.

In the meantime, Roy had been hard at work on the door of the *lager*. We were locked in every night, and although the bolt was on the outside, the nuts were on our side, inside the room. Roy had been patiently loosening the nuts for a while, with the assistance of a spanner from the farm where he worked. But there was one hitch. If we tried to push the door, it was possible the catch on the door would fall apart, making a real din, and alerting the guards. Roy seemed to have an answer to every problem, and he managed to get his hands on a bit of wire, which he fed through a narrow gap at the top of the door, to support the catch and prevent it from dropping to the floor noisily.

With all the necessary arrangements in place, the big day was looming. Roy and I went to the storeroom to get the supplies we'd stashed away. We couldn't believe it. There was nothing there. It had all gone. We just couldn't understand it: where had all our stuff gone?

I had my suspicions, however. Next door to the camp lived a woman with five children. Had the youngsters come across the food and taken it? We called at the house, and we could tell by the mother's face that she knew exactly why we were there. She apologised straightaway and said the children had spotted the food after they'd gone into the storeroom when they were playing outside.

'Don't worry,' she said. 'I have got everything here for

you,' as she reached behind her. And there it was: our stash of food in the bag. Or, at least, most of it. There were a few notable absentees. Temptation had got the better of the children and some of the chocolate bars had been devoured.

Having recovered our supplies, there was no more time to waste. The much anticipated and planned-for hour of departure had finally arrived.

This brings me back to the chopped onions in water, because it was now time to put them to good use. We'd got hold of some old sacks on the farms where we worked, and we'd immersed those in the concoction of onions and water. We then wore them over our boots so that the smell of onions would put the guard dogs off our scent.

The three of us seemed all set. Then, at the very last moment, there was a change of plan. Len Caulfield decided he was pulling out. He didn't want to risk it. That was fair enough. It was better he pulled out before we started than change his mind when we were already on the run. We'd always thought it would be easier to flee as a pair. But there was yet another twist. Joe Walker, hearing that Len was not going with us, wanted to come instead. This placed us in an awkward position: it was hard to say 'No' to someone who was so keen to join us. So, after a bit of deliberation we agreed to let Joe come with us.

On a cold night in early December 1943 we left the *lager*. Thank God, the door opened quickly and quietly. We were out. It was my first taste of real freedom in two-and-a-half years, and it was very sweet.

Under the moonlight we made our way towards the Pinka river, past the fields where Roy and I had first met a few months earlier. Our aim was to follow the river up to the bridge. But someone had placed a bundle of telegraph poles along the path, and in the darkness we hit them. All three of us had a bit of a jolt, and we thought the resulting noise was sure to alert the German guards. Fortunately it didn't, and on we went.

Our initial plan then was to go under the bridge, but Roy had another thought. 'Hang on,' he said. 'I don't think there's anyone on the bridge.' We thought there would be enemy soldiers there, but luckily, there was no sign of them. It seemed safe to go, and we ran across the bridge as fast as we could.

We had just made it to the other side of the bridge when we heard something. People walking, we thought. The noise came from behind us. Near the bridge lay a gutter, a couple of feet deep, and we jumped down into it. As luck would have it, a large cloud spread over the moon at that very moment, and darkness fell instantly. And at exactly the same time it also started to snow.

We could see some figures coming over the bridge and they had at least one dog with them. We thought our escape was over almost as soon as it had begun. We were sure that we would be spotted and caught. We stood exactly where we were. In the gutter. No one dared move. The footsteps got nearer and nearer, and then, ever so gradually, faded away. What a relief!

After composing ourselves, we now had to get back

on track. We ventured on, making our way through some fields. But it was so dark, we couldn't see properly where we were going. We were following our noses and trusting our luck.

The snow continued to fall, which made it quite slippery underfoot. Suddenly a door was thrown open door and a light flashed. We threw ourselves to the ground instinctively and immediately. We were within ten yards of a sentry box, where at least one German soldier and a dog were stationed. There was no sign of the dog, but we could see the soldier quite clearly. We just hoped to God that he couldn't see us or sense there was someone watching him. After a few seconds, which lasted so much longer, he turned and went back into the sentry box. We knew exactly where we were now. We were actually on the border between Austria and Hungary.

But there was still another checkpoint to negotiate before we were safely across the border. In the distance we could make out a Hungarian soldier outside his sentry box. And we could see his dog, too. Very soon it began to bark. And that barking just wouldn't stop. The soldier had the dog on some kind of lead, and he shouted at the animal, urging it to stop. I've no doubt the old dog could sense there were people nearby. Fortunately, the soldier wasn't as canny as his canine companion. He must have decided it was too cold to stand outside in the snow, and made his way back into the sentry box.

Once he was inside we made a run for it, and we were across the border in no time. The aim now was to travel as far as we could under the cover of darkness. What a night! But the first few hurdles had been successfully negotiated, and it was a start. We had found freedom. Hanging on to that freedom would prove more problematic.

# On the Run

As we made our way through Hungary, all three of us agreed that we should keep heading east as far as we could, before turning south towards Yugoslavia. That was the plan, at least. Roy had a little stud in his shirt with a compass in it. Before we started each day's travelling, we would confer with the compass to check which direction we were heading. Our problem was that once we were underway we couldn't really look at the compass because we were moving under cover of darkness. We chose to do that because it meant there was less chance of us being seen and rounded up and taken back to a Nazi camp.

We came to a large forest. We thought this was ideal, as it gave us even more shelter. We would carry on walking through the night until sunrise every morning. Then we would stop, and eat some of the ever diminishing stock of food we had taken with us. We had been trying to follow the path of a river. But that river meandered, of course, and when it seemed that we had crossed it, it would come back to meet us again. After a few days on the run, we sensed it was a strategy which confused more than it helped us.

I remember one night we came to a point where we

wanted to cross the river. But, in the moonlight, the water looked deep and the current strong. From the river bank Roy looked down. 'I know it looks pretty deep, but we're going to have to cross somewhere around here,' he said. 'I'll go in first to see how deep it is, and where it would be best for us to try to cross.'

Okay, we thought, let's give it a go. And that's what happened. In the cold winter weather Roy took his clothes off, and into the river he ventured. Within a couple of steps he was almost out of sight. The water was much deeper than he'd predicted.

'Oh, no. It's too deep,' he said. 'I'm going to have to come out.'

So we modified our plans, and carried on walking along the river bank until we came to a more suitable place to cross. But unfortunately we couldn't find such a spot. So we stopped in a place where the bulrushes grew high above us. At least we could get some shelter there and some well-earned rest. There was no way anyone could find us there.

Roy loved his smoke, as many soldiers did during the war, and he now decided that the time was right to light up and enjoy a cigarette. I told him not to. Even if people couldn't see us, they would see the smoke and smell the cigarette fumes. There was a danger our plans could, almost literally, go up in smoke. Roy, as mentioned earlier, was very determined and highly inventive. So desperate was he to light up that he pulled his overcoat over his head to contain the smoke before puffing away to his heart's content. Within a few minutes, however, he started scratching himself. 'Oh no, boys,' he said. 'I think I've got lice crawling all over me.'

'I wouldn't be surprised if they've been drawn by the smoke,' I told him. 'Stay away from us,' said Joe, as we laughed at Roy's uncomfortable predicament.

It's odd how some things come unexpectedly to mind. At that moment I was transported back to Murau in the shadow of the Austrian Alps where I had been over a year earlier. There an Australian POW named George East had itched and scratched like Roy, fearing he had lice in his pubic hair. He had obtained some kind of powder which was supposed to get rid of the lice, and I remember him taking all his clothes off and rubbing the powder over his genitals. We couldn't believe what happened next. Poor old George must have used far too much of this miracle cure. Within seconds he was leaping about madly, shouting and screaming, and saying his genitals were on fire. Seeing him jump around brought out the worst in his fellow POWs. We laughed so much we had tears in our eyes. George, of course, was in too much pain to see the funny side. It took him a while to calm down, and I never saw him use the lice powder again.

In Hungary, however, there was more at stake. We had to find a way of dealing quickly with the lice problem. Despite the freezing temperature, we all stripped off and turned our clothes inside out. Our reasoning was that the cold weather would kill the lice there and then. And, boy, was it cold! Biting cold. It just took our breath away. Joe was screaming. 'It's too bloody cold. I've got to put my clothes back on,' he said. 'This is killing me.'

I don't think any of us had dressed so quickly in our lives. Looking back, I don't believe any of us had been infested with lice. But Roy had started to contemplate the possibility, and the itching began. In extreme conditions, where you're cold and tired, your mind starts playing tricks. And I'm quite sure that's what happened with Roy.

We carried on walking for a few nights after that, and caught up with some sleep in the day. At last we reached a point where we could now cross the river. There was a bridge in front of us. But there was nothing ordinary about it. It had a very ornate design, resembling some kind of aristocratic folly. Roy was the first to cross, and when he got to the other side he whistled to signal it was safe for Joe and me to follow.

We had kept away from villages and houses since our escape, and our main enemy now was the weather. The nights were bitterly cold. We decided we needed to find some shelter and longed to be indoors. Soon we came to a little farm, and our hope was to rest a while in one of the outbuildings. As we approached the farm entrance, we saw a large dog coming towards us. It didn't bark, but stared at us, fixing his gaze menacingly. The three of us decided it would be best not to try to pass the dog. So, we turned back, and put our plans to rest on the back burner.

It wasn't long before we came to another farm. Everything seemed quiet, so we made our way towards one of the outbuildings. There was a ladder up to the loft, and up we went. It was an ideal place to sleep for a few hours, we thought. But we had only been up there a few minutes when Joe decided to go down to answer the call of nature.

A few seconds later the door flew open. A man came in, collected some chaff, and went out again, without seeing Joe standing behind the door. He came back up the ladder to where Roy and I were lying down. In less than ten minutes the chaff man was back again. And without a word of a lie, he placed his hand where Joe had peed. Realising that he had urine all over his hand, the man scolded his dog, thinking that it was responsible for the damp patch. When he went out and shut the door, the three of us enjoyed a good old laugh, albeit a quiet one.

We stayed there overnight and slept well. In the morning, as we peered out, we could see people going back and forth from one of the smaller buildings. We came to the conclusion that there must have been a little dairy there. We decided that I would stand guard whilst Roy and Joe would go over and get us some milk.

As they entered the dairy, they were met by the wonderful aroma of freshly baked bread. They spotted seven or eight loaves on a little bench. Joe grabbed a couple and made a sharp exit before we all made a run for it. Within a few minutes we found ourselves in a forest eating chunks of fresh bread. It was lovely. I can almost smell and taste that bread now. There was something very special about the sharing of the bread in the silence of the forest. It almost had echoes of Holy Communion.

With some fuel in our stomachs, on we went. We

wandered through the forest for a couple of days, thinking that we were heading towards Yugoslavia. Eventually we came across a huge pile of neatly cut wood, and could hear the sound of chopping. Joe went to find out what was going on. He came back and said he could see an elderly man splitting wood. He had a horse and cart with him. Roy suggested that we should go over and offer the man some help, in return for directions to Yugoslavia. I wasn't so sure. I was worried the man would smell a rat and tell the authorities. But I was outvoted by the other two, and we approached the man in the forest.

When he saw us, he jumped a little. Despite the language barrier, however, he quickly understood that we were offering our help, and he welcomed our services. Roy and I helped him split the wood, and Joe lifted the blocks into the cart. Joe then accompanied him back to his farm, and they came back within an hour or so with a supply of food – bread, cheese and some kind of meat.

After working with the farmer in the forest for another couple of hours, he invited us to his home, where he lived with his wife and two daughters. As we enjoyed a meal with them, we chatted as best we could. The farmer's wife was very friendly, as was the youngest daughter. But the eldest girl seemed more on edge. She was obviously suspicious of us.

The farmer and his wife said the three of us could stay overnight in one of their outbuildings. As the farmer showed us where we would be sleeping, Joe went outside to answer yet another of his calls of nature. He hadn't been gone long when he rushed back in to tell us that he had just seen the eldest daughter run towards the village. We all agreed it was likely she was going to squeal on us. It was time to leave.

As we made our way through the shelter of the forest, we saw the daughter in the distance coming back towards us with two men in uniform. I don't think they could see us as we were sheltered by a line of trees. But our fears had been confirmed. By now the three of us had been on the run for the best part of two weeks. We were tired. But we couldn't give up now. There was no choice but to carry on.

We had been on the move all night, and by the morning Joe said he'd had enough. 'I can't go on,' he said. 'My legs have given up. You two go on. I'm going to stay here, and if I'm caught then that's it, I'll say I've been on my own, and I won't mention you two at all.'

But Roy and I managed to persuade Joe to persevere for a while yet, and on we went again. A couple of hours down the line, Roy collapsed in pain. This was very unusual. Roy was as strong as the proverbial ox. But there was something wrong, he was very pale and complained that he had a stomach bug. He may have been suffering the ill effects of some frozen swedes he had eaten in a field a few hours before.

Whatever the cause, we had no option. We had to rest for a while and hope Roy would get better soon, so that we could move on again. We managed to find a little spot in the forest where we could rest. We lit a fire there, filled our tins with snow and warmed them to make some tea.

We hadn't had time for more than a few sips of tea when we heard voices coming towards us. In no time we were surrounded. There must have been over 20 people around us, mostly foresters, but there were two men in uniform as well. We had been caught. We were escorted to the nearest village where there were police and soldiers waiting for us.

The next morning we were put on a train. Once again, we didn't know where we were going or what was ahead of us. But what we did know was that our brief period of freedom had come to an impromptu end.

# Behind Bars

We had been on the train for hours, but we were none the wiser as to where we were heading. Initially, we thought we were going towards the city of Budapest. But, when the train stopped about 50 miles short of the Hungarian capital, we were told to make our way out. We had reached a place called Komárom, close to the border with Czechoslovakia. We were far from Yugoslavia, where we had hoped to get to after escaping from Gaas in Austria. The train had brought us to northern Hungary; the border with Yugoslavia was right down in the south. There was nothing we could do about that. We weren't masters of our own destiny.

From Komárom station, Hungarian soldiers marched us up to an old castle. One look at this place was enough to know that there would be very little solace here. The stench hit us as we walked through the main gates. It was a filthy place.

Very soon the three of us found ourselves in a cell. What an experience that was. It was crawling with insects, most of them large ones. I hadn't seen anything like it. There were several prisoners in the cell already, and straw was spread thinly over the stone floor. By the look of it, the straw had been there for a while. It was rotten. I didn't really want to think what was mixed in it, but I knew one thing: I wasn't intending to sit on it or touch it.

We were now under the supervision of the Hungarian military authorities, rather than the Nazis. In 1943 it was a complicated political situation because the Hungarians had been on the Germans' side in the war, but many influential people in the country wanted to change that, and support the Allies.

Whilst the three of us had been on the run in the forests of Hungary, we had discussed what we would say if we were caught. So we knew what we would tell the authorities. Because we were all ordinary soldiers, without rank, we had decided one of us would have to assume officer status if we were apprehended. POWs were treated far better if they had an officer amongst them.

Roy wanted me to be the officer. But I believed it made more sense for Roy to play that part. It would be more difficult for the enemy to check out the credentials of a soldier from New Zealand than one from Britain. And that's what happened. In a mock ceremony in a Hungarian forest, we had awarded Roy a commission as a 'Captain'. I don't know what the King's response would have been, but he wasn't there to voice any objections!

When the authorities at Komárom realised one of us was an 'officer', their attitude towards us changed considerably. 'I'm sorry,' said one of the guards as he spoke to Roy. 'I didn't understand you were an officer.'

Soon we were moved from the large, stinking communal cell. Joe and I found ourselves in a cell for two, and Roy, because he was an 'officer', was afforded a little more space on his own. Our new quarters were undoubtedly an improvement on what we had before, but they were still quite dirty and unpleasant.

There were dozens of other prisoners at the old castle. Why they were there, and where they'd all come from, I don't really know, but they seemed to be drawn from a host of different nations. Many were dressed in rags with nothing on their feet. Quite a few of the inmates were Russians and Poles. Because there was a cross-section of nationalities there, arguments and fights happened on a regular basis. There was no sign of a united nations spirit at Komárom. The disagreements escalated quickly into nasty affairs. Punches were thrown, kicks landed, and there was hair-pulling, shouting and screaming. We made sure we stayed out of these stormy altercations, and kept our heads down.

The most difficult thing about being locked up anywhere is the loss of freedom. That is what got to me, more than anything. Though I would never consider myself a poet, during our time at Komárom I did start composing poems in Welsh. It just helped concentrate my mind, and I think it gave me some kind of inner strength and a connection with home. As I sat in a soul-destroying cell in a Hungarian jail, it was essential for me to maintain the belief that I would one day return to my family and friends in Carmarthenshire.

After a few days Roy came to visit Joe and me in our cell. With him were two guards, one of whom spoke English. He'd come to tell us we could be on the move again shortly. He didn't know where or when. Another couple of days passed, and the same guard instructed us to go with him. He didn't give us much information, but he said he thought we were to be transferred to a prison in Budapest.

Leaving Komárom was a relief at least, but once we got to the prison in the Hungarian capital, we realised this was another grim place. As we made our way along the corridors, we could look into the cells. The prisoners were like caged animals in a zoo. It was very noisy. I don't know whether we were being welcomed or scorned, but I found the whole atmosphere quite demoralizing.

Roy's perceived officer status meant that he was again kept apart from Joe and myself. But, three days later, Roy visited us with the obligatory Hungarian guards, of course. They had exciting news. We were to be transported to the Swiss Embassy in Budapest, which handled matters related to British subjects in wartime Hungary.

Once we arrived there, we had a chance to enjoy a proper wash, and rid ourselves of the odours and grime of the prisons in Komárom and Budapest. When we were dry and dressed, we were joined by three other British soldiers, all Scots. They, like us, were escapees who'd been caught and imprisoned again. A deputation of very official, important-looking people then arrived to speak to us. One of those was a man of the cloth, the Very Reverend Alexander Szent-Iványi, Deputy Bishop of the Unitarian Church in Hungary. He spoke excellent English, albeit with an American accent. His wife, apparently, hailed from the United States.

He outlined what lay ahead of us. We were going to be on

the move yet again. This time our destination was a place in southern Hungary, about 20 miles from the Yugoslavian border, a place called Szigetvár. There we would be based on a large estate, belonging to a Count, one Graf Andrassy Mihaly. The Deputy Bishop explained that we wouldn't be prisoners in the traditional sense – we wouldn't be kept in cells and so forth – but we wouldn't have total freedom either. We would 'assist Hungary' he said, and we would have to respect the country's people and traditions and way of life. We were expected to work on the estate, in return for our bed and board. More than anything, said Szent-Iványi, we would need to be 'careful', that was the message. But he said he couldn't give us any further details at that time.

After the meeting with the Deputy Bishop and his colleagues, we walked out into the Budapest evening. What a great feeling that was. The scene is vivid in my mind's eye now. It was late December 1943, and it had been snowing heavily. The streets were covered in a greying slush as the snow melted. We weren't free men, of course, because there were four or five Hungarian soldiers accompanying us, watching every move. But at least we could get a good old lungful of fresh air once again as we walked towards the train station in Budapest.

There was a little café at the station. We went there to sit and wait for our train to Szigetvár. We didn't have any money on us, of course, but the café owner came over with a coffee each for Joe, Roy and myself in a simple, but kind gesture.

We weren't the only people in that little station café. On a table next to us there were several Cigani, Hungary's Romany gypsies. They had some musical instruments, and I particularly remember the violinists who were obviously very gifted musicians. When they realised we were Allied soldiers, they began playing some tunes especially for us. There was one song in particular, which was extremely popular before the war, called 'South of the Border'. I remember the words to this day:

> South of the border,
> Down Mexico way.
> That's where I fell in love
> And the stars above came out to play.

And as the Cigani played, we sang along. It was such a heartwarming experience. I'll never forget it. But the train arrived to put an end to the singing.

As we made our way down to Szigetvár, the snow was falling heavily. The train stopped every now and again, not just in the stations, but in other places as well. It may have been because there was snow on the tracks, I don't know. Roy saw this as an opportunity. He reached over and whispered in my ear, 'The next time the trains stops, I'm going to get out and run for it.'

'Don't be silly,' I told him. 'Look, Roy, this train is moving in the right direction for us. It's going down south, towards Yugoslavia. It's where we want to go.' Somehow I managed to persuade my Kiwi friend to stay on the train.

A few hours later we arrived in Szigetvár. As we stepped off the train, there were more soldiers waiting for us, this time to take us up to the estate. Because the authorities believed Roy was a Captain, he was allowed to stay at the Graf's mansion, 'Graf' being the Hungarian for 'Count'. The estate owner Graf Andrassy Mihaly didn't speak English, but he was fluent in German. As I had a smattering of German, I was granted permission to stay near the mansion as well. Joe and the other boys had to make do with the stable block. But even the stables were quite plush. They weren't what you would find on the average Hungarian farm.

The Graf was a very rich and powerful man. As well as the Szigetvár estate, he owned another one in South Africa, and some other properties elsewhere across the world. He was also an important political figure.

There must have been about 20 POWs on the estate, and we were all given different tasks. The Graf was very progressive in his attitude towards life and work. In many ways he was a man well ahead of his time. Those who worked at his mills, including our boys, were allowed to receive medical treatments, X-rays and the like, at a medical centre he had set up locally. There was a hospital he had established nearby as well, employing doctors who had all been trained in Germany. The Graf contributed generously to the running of these places. He used his wealth for the benefit of the whole community.

We sensed Szigetvár was a good place to live and work. It was such a fascinating town. I must admit I was captivated by the place and some of the things I saw there. I remember being extremely impressed after witnessing what was a very unusual sight for someone like me brought up in a rural area. There was a man whose role was to look after pigs. Every morning, at the break of dawn, he would set off with his horn and his little whip. He would walk through the town blowing the horn, and people would let their pigs out. The animals would then follow the man to a field on the outskirts of the town, where they would spend their days happily eating and rolling around. In the evenings the man would bring the pigs back to the town, and each of them would go home to the very same place they'd left in the morning. They knew exactly where to go. If I hadn't seen it myself, I wouldn't have believed it. It was quite a sight.

One evening Roy visited my room. He was obviously excited. 'You'll never believe it, mate,' he said. 'I've been invited to dinner with the Count. But since I haven't got any German, I've asked if you can come along to help with the translating.'

The arrangement was that Roy, as the 'officer' would go there for the dinner itself, and I was to join them once they had finished their food. And that's what happened. The Graf welcomed me heartily. Not only did he want me to translate Roy's words, he was also keen to talk to me about my life and my background, in German, of course.

After a while the butler came in, with a box of cigars. He offered the Graf the first one, then he went to Roy, and finally me. I'd never smoked a cigar in my life, but I didn't want to show the Graf that I wasn't worldly wise. I'd seen a few films where these American cowboys would bite off the top of the cigar, and spit it out, before lighting up. So, I thought I would copy those film stars, and I bit the top of the cigar and spat it out. The next thing I knew, the butler was back with some kind of tool to cut off the top for us. I wasn't sure what I should do with the chunk I'd bitten off, so I dropped it down on the floor next to me. The Graf had a big dog, and it wandered over and sat near me. I looked down and saw it was chewing the piece of cigar I had discarded. Within a few seconds the dog started coughing and spluttering. It wouldn't stop. The Graf then reached for his bell and called the butler. 'Take that dog out,' he said in German. 'I don't know what the hell is wrong with it.'

Of course, I knew only too well what had caused the dog's coughing fit, but I decided to keep my counsel. We went on to enjoy a pleasurable evening with the Graf. When the dog came back in later, I decided it would be best to keep out of its way.

Without a doubt, the relaxed atmosphere at Szigetvár was very different to anything I'd experienced since being captured on the island of Crete two-and-a-half years earlier. But I suspected there was quite a specific reason why we, as a group of POWs, had been chosen to come to this big estate in southern Hungary. By the beginning of 1944 we would get to know more about the task that lay ahead of us.

# 'Top Secret' Plans

We welcomed a new year with the visit of a familiar face. In early 1944 the Very Reverend Alexander Szent-Iványi arrived in Szigetvár. He was someone we trusted. He had been so good to us and other POWs. The Unitarian Deputy Bishop had come down from Budapest principally to see Roy, as our 'officer'. The clergyman's intention was to shed more light on the role we were to play over the next few weeks.

Szent-Ivanyi instructed Roy that the mission we were to be part of was 'top secret'. Information was provided on a need-to-know basis, and it wasn't to go on beyond our tight-knit circle. A few of us were called in to hear what Szent-Ivanyi had to say. 'The British government is trying to get the Hungarian government to support the Allied war effort, and come out against the Germans,' he said, as everyone in the room listened closely. 'There's a lot going on in the background at the moment and what we have in mind is that a deputation of very influential people will be landing here by parachute one night. We want you to arrange the place of landing and then escort the deputation up to Budapest. It's imperative that no one else outside this room finds out about this.'

We were all somewhat taken aback by Szent-Iványi's words. And I must admit to having some reservations about the plans. But, because the information had been shared amongst so few of us, we had to be careful about discussing things. Our group of POWs was drawn from all kinds of nations. I've already mentioned the Scots, there were also boys from countries like Canada, Australia and New Zealand, not to mention a few Englishmen, of course.

There was one exceptionally interesting character in our midst, a French Jew called Henry Lowenstein. Extremely able, he spoke many languages, but his greatest accomplishment was his ability to forge documents. He could make copies of official documents that would look every bit as authentic as the originals. There was another Jewish man in the group as well, whom we called Tom Sanders. I doubt whether that was his real name, because he was Hungarian, and he, again, could speak many different languages. Because he spoke the native language, he was selected as a kind of go-between, someone who could collect information about important developments and relay it quickly to the rest of us. He was particularly useful to Roy who needed to be briefed regularly on the news that was coming from Budapest.

As 'Captain', Roy would travel frequently on the train between Szigetvár and the Hungarian capital. He would have regular discussions with a man called Colonel Howie, who had escaped from a Nazi camp and played a key role in the plans to try to bring these people of influence over from London.

As regards the parachute landing, we had been instructed to go to a spot about half-a-mile outside Szigetvár. We would all be given torches, and the plan was for the plane to come down to 1,500 feet until they saw the light shining from our torches: that light would be its guide. The key personnel on the plane would then be parachuted down. Our role then was to collect their parachutes, whilst they themselves would be escorted by Roy and Tom Sanders on the train up to Budapest.

The landing was supposed to happen towards the end of January 1944. Everything seemed to be in place and we were all ready to go. But, the day before it was supposed to happen, Szent-Iványi came down to Szigetvár to tell us it had been postponed. Another date and time would be arranged and we would be informed in due course. Within a couple of weeks we had another visit from the Deputy Bishop, this time accompanied by his wife. They brought a wireless down for us, so that we could listen for signals.

One night when one of our boys was listening to the radio, I heard a shout. 'Dai, come here quick,' he said excitedly. 'Come and listen to this, come and listen. I think there's a programme from Wales on the wireless!'

In the 1940s there was a very well-known variety programme on the wireless. Its name escapes me, but this particular broadcast featured a tenor-and-baritone duet, Towyn Harries and Idris Daniels. They were from the Llandeilo area in Carmarthenshire, and I knew them both! Towyn was a fantastic tenor who had won at the National

Eisteddfod, and Idris had a wonderfully rich baritone voice. I couldn't believe it. There I was in Hungary listening to the radio and hearing these two men, whom I knew from home, singing in Welsh. It was a very surreal moment, and one which made the hair on the back of my neck stand on end. It's difficult to explain, but that simple experience filled my heart with joy.

After spending several weeks in Szigetvár, the boys began to grow restless. Some wanted to try to get out and make their way to Yugoslavia, since the border was only about 20 miles away. Of course, only a small group of us actually knew about Szent-Iványi's plans. Luckily, Roy managed to convince those who wanted to leave to stay, for the time being at least.

We needed to utilise Henry Lowenstein's forging skills to make passports. We went to a photography shop in Szigetvár where two Jewish women very kindly took our pictures, free of charge. Lowenstein then made up passports for us. We were given those so that we had 'official documents' if we were stopped by the authorities at any time.

In the meantime a new date was arranged for the parachute landing. It was to be in February but, frustratingly, when February came and everyone was ready, it was postponed yet again. We would have to wait once more for another date. Then, on 19 March, 1944, something happened which would put an end to the long-awaited mission.

In the early hours of that morning we heard enemy planes in the sky: the Germans were preparing to invade

Hungary. I think the Nazis had found out our intention to bring in these influential people from London, and the plans to support Britain and the Allies. The German invasion of Hungary would have been too much of a coincidence, otherwise.

At the time we were in Szigetvár, the estate manager was a German. Despite the fact that Graf Andrassy Mihaly welcomed us with open arms, the manager never liked us POWs, and made it absolutely clear from our arrival that he didn't approve of us being there. I wouldn't be at all surprised if he had got to know about Szent-Iványi's plans somehow, and passed information on to the Nazi authorities.

In no time we were rounded up by a large contingent of German soldiers. All the POWs were locked in a room on the estate. The Germans refused to give us any information about what was going to happen to us, or where we were to be taken.

At the back of the room we had spotted a little door. We made a noise to distract the German soldiers, whilst a few of us tried to prise the door open. But it wouldn't open fully, creating a gap of only a few inches.

Among the POWs from New Zealand, there was one called Sammy Hoare. His full name was Allen Hugh Hoare, but we called him 'Sammy'. He was a quiet chap, very unassuming, and a bit of a thinker, but he was more than prepared to play his part when called upon. Sammy was as thin as a rake, and some of the boys managed to push him out through the tiny gap in the door. On the other side, Sammy pulled the door a few inches more, so that there was room for another person to get out. We quickly decided amongst ourselves that Roy should be that man, because he knew more about what was going on in Budapest than anyone else. And if the Germans got to know that he had been liaising with people like Colonel Howie in the Hungarian capital, Roy would be in deep trouble. So out he went. As he made for the door, the Germans spotted him and started firing. But he had an advantage of a second or two over the gunmen, and he managed to sneak through unharmed. He then ran as fast as he could and got away.

The rest of us weren't so lucky. We were all put on a train to Siklós, less than 20 miles from Szigetvár. The prison there was a horrible place, as we had long come to expect. Whilst we were there, one of our boys, Joe Burke, tried to escape. The Englishman tied some old blankets together to form a makeshift rope, and tried to abseil down from a high window. Unfortunately, the blankets unravelled and Joe fell 30 feet to the ground, and broke his leg. But despite the outcome of that incident, Joe wasn't the only one to try to escape from Siklós.

Every day a horse and cart came through the main gates to collect refuse. One day, I spotted a golden opportunity to flee. As the cart came in, I rolled under it and got out of the gates. I thought I'd made it. Unbelievably, the horse decided to stop in its tracks to empty its bowels, and I was spotted, caught, and manhandled back into my cell.

As things turned out, I didn't have to stay there for long. Within a matter of days we were on another train, on a journey that would take us out of Hungary. And, if we thought things were bad in Siklós, they were about to get a whole lot worse.

# Hell on Earth

Our journey from Siklós came to an end in Belgrade, capital city of Yugoslavia. Since escaping from Gaas in Austria, my aim had been to reach Yugoslavia. But I wanted to get there a free man. The reality was very different. I was there as a prisoner of war.

We were taken to a place called Zemun. This was a Nazi concentration camp on the outskirts of Belgrade. Without a shadow of doubt, it was the most awful place I had ever seen. Yes, I'd been held in pretty miserable places before. But they were nothing like this. Everywhere else paled into insignificance compared to Zemun.

It was difficult to comprehend what happened there and what would happen. It is absolutely impossible to describe Zemun to anyone who hasn't been there, felt it, and smelled it. For me, this was quite simply hell on earth.

The Nazis' name for Zemun was Semlin, and it was located on the site of the old Belgrade Exhibition Grounds. There were several large buildings there known as pavilions. The Nazis had first taken people there to be incarcerated in 1941. At that time it was a *Judenlager*, a camp where Jewish people were imprisoned. Thousands of Jews had been taken there, men, women and children. They weren't guilty of any crimes, of course. They were simply taken there because they were Jews, and Hitler hated them. And the horrible truth was that once the Jews arrived at Zemun, there was very little chance they would leave alive.

The Nazis had these gas vans, also known as death vans. Cruelly, they would pile about 80 to 100 Jews at a time, including elderly people and young children, into the back of large vans, and they would expose them to a poisonous gas which would kill them. Can you imagine such a thing? Apparently, 6,300 Jews were killed at Zemun between March and May 1942. That was just cold-blooded, inhuman cruelty.

After they had killed almost every single Jew to enter Zemun, the Nazis changed the camp's status. From the middle of 1942 onwards it became an *Anhaltelager*, a camp where political prisoners were held. These were mostly Partisans from Yugoslavia, who now supported the Allies in the war. In truth, these people weren't politically active. They were just ordinary Serbians from different parts of Yugoslavia. Many of them had just helped Partisan soldiers by offering them food or giving them shelter overnight, whilst several of them were just families and old people who happened to live in villages where there was support for the Partisans. They weren't guilty of any real crimes.

By the time we reched Zemun in March 1944 there were people of all ages and backgrounds there, many of them women and children. There were some Jewish people as well, but not many.

In the block where we were held, there wasn't even a

roof over our heads. To all intents and purposes, we were outdoors, exposed to the elements. In terms of hygiene and sanitation it was awful. I can't remember seeing a single toilet there, and it stank. It was absolutely disgusting. The stench was unlike anything I'd come across before – a potent mixture of the worst odours of life mixed with the unmistakable, lingering aroma of death.

As you can imagine, there was very little food, and what we were given was incredibly bad. I remember a very weak cabbage soup, which looked like dirty water and tasted even worse. There was the odd scrap of stale bread, and tiny amounts of water. But there was nothing that was remotely nourishing. Nothing. People were starving there. Every single day there were several deaths. People were just dying on their feet.

There were scenes of unfathomable cruelty. I remember one day seeing a woman with a baby queuing for some food and holding a small bowl. When she got the front, she was given a few drops of that horrible cabbage soup. Starving, she turned to the officer, and asked if she could have some more. But, instead of giving the young mother an extra spoonful, the officer knocked the bowl out of her hand and laughed in her face. Those of us waiting behind the woman were incensed by what we saw, and it was only the presence of heavily armed guards that prevented a riot. The sad truth was, though, that no one could really challenge these guards. Such bravery would have been folly: we would probably have been shot dead there and then.

The only way we could help the young mother was by offering her some of the contents of our own meagre bowls. The poor woman didn't get much, but it was better than nothing, and it was some kind of moral support.

They treated us like dirt. I find it impossible to fully describe how bad things were. The guards used their guns as punishment sticks, and prisoners were hit in their stomachs, on their backs, even in their faces. And there were some assaults more brutal than these as inmates were punched and kicked to within an inch of their lives. They really were heart-rending scenes.

It was little wonder that many lost their heads in such an atmosphere. Some poor desperate souls would run at the large wire fences and try to clamber over. Such attempts were futile, however. As they struggled to gain footholds on the fence, they were unceremoniously shot in the back. Very often the guards would leave their bodies there to decay, a reminder and warning to others who harboured similar thoughts of escape. The message was clear and stark. There was no way out.

We were kept in the block with no roof for several days, before a dozen or so of us were moved to another area of the camp. It was marginally better, but still very unpleasant. There we met up with half a dozen Americans. One of the boys who had been moved with me was a Canadian, Norman McLean. I had first met him at the estate in Szigetvár, Hungary. I'm not sure why but most of us knew him as 'Roy'. That was a bit confusing, because we had another Roy in the group at Szigetvár, our 'Captain', Roy

Natusch from New Zealand. Anyway, Norman McLean and I got on well. From Szigetvár, we had gone on to Siklós and now Zemun together. He was full of beans, and a key member of our group because he always found a way to keep our spirits up, even in the darkest of times. At Zemun he was a lifeline.

As far as I could judge, Norman's only flaw was that he could sometimes be too enthusiastic and adventurous. There were occasions when we would have to hold him back, for his own good. But he was a man you could depend on. He had been a member of the Canadian Commandos when he was captured by the Germans in 1942, and was one of the bravest men I'd ever met, a real daredevil.

I wasn't surprised, therefore, when he came to me one day with an idea. 'I've been thinking about things and I believe we could get through this fence, you know,' he said. 'I think there could be a way out. Are you willing to give it a go with me?'

'Certainly,' I said. I didn't have to think too much about it. I'd had enough of Zemun. Everything about the place turned my stomach. One night we wandered over to inspect the fence to see what lay ahead of us. Initially, we thought it reached the ground and ended there. We were wrong. It had been sunk quite deep into the earth, a foot or so down, at a guess. It was obvious that escaping would be a hell of task. But Norman and I weren't people who baulked at a challenge. On the plus side, the earth was very sandy, not like the rock-like Austrian clay at the brickworks in Knittelfeld two years before. So we decided we would dig as much as we could with our hands, just to see how deep we could go. Norman started to scratch the sand, gradually piling it up behind him for me to scatter. Then we would swap roles to give each other some respite. When we caught glimpse of a guard, we moved away swiftly. It was a very slow process, and we had to be patient. On the third evening of digging, the guards were out in force, and we had to abort our plans. I think someone must have told them they suspected we were trying to dig our way out. But, to be honest, as difficult as it was to admit defeat, without any cutters or similar tools, I don't think we would have been able to get out under the fence anyway.

However the horrors of Zemun fed the urge to escape. We were treated like wild animals, and the Nazis weren't the only perpetrators of pain at the camp. The Croatian guards at Zemun were just as bad. They seemed to have no qualms about striking poor defenceless people. Though both peoples hailed from the same country, the Croats and the Serbs hated each other. The conflict between them further complicated the fragile political situation in wartime Yugoslavia. Those tensions surfaced again in the 1990s, of course, and the consequences were devastating. But, in 1944, it was the Nazis who ruled the roost at Zemun. They gave the orders which led to countless acts of cruelty.

We were soon to find ourselves under attack from above, as well. On 16 April, 1944, the midday skies echoed to the sound of American aircraft dropping bombs on Belgrade. The huge blasts shook everything to its core. Zemun was

## Hell on Earth

targeted because there was a railway and an airport nearby. The bombing went on for two days, and the RAF took part in the attack on the second day. At night, between each volley of bombs, there were searchlights in the air and the sky was bright white.

How we survived as bombs fell continually around us, I just don't know. Not everyone shared our luck, however. There were four soldiers from South Africa a few yards away from us, and they had terror in their eyes. All four were desperately trying to dig a slit trench to seek shelter from the aerial onslaught. By the second day, however, that trench was a crater. We never saw them again.

Between 16 and 17 April it is believed that at least 200 people at Zemun were killed by the bombs. Many fear the true figure could be much higher. Several buildings on the site of the camp were destroyed, and hundreds were injured. And many of those injuries were truly awful. It was common to see people who'd had a leg blown off, others had arms actually hanging loosely from their bodies. There were some who had horrendous wounds to their stomachs and sides. People were crawling on the floor, begging for mercy. I never saw anything like it.

And I never heard anything like the groaning. The high-pitched groaning. That got to me, too. It was the sound of unspeakable pain, and it could be heard day and night. It was as if the casualties were calling out to someone, anyone. A desperate plea for help, perhaps, for someone to come and tend their wounds? Or were they pleas to God, to be put out of their misery? It was difficult to believe any god was listening, however, such was the scale of the suffering. I had never heard sounds like these before, and thankfully, I haven't heard them since either. They were bone-chilling.

Over the years, war films have tried to re-create harrowing scenes of conflict in different ways. But, I can tell you now, if someone hasn't been there, in one of these horrible situations, it is absolutely impossible to understand how dreadful it was. I just can't put it into words.

There is no doubt that the bombing and its effects were devastating. But, for me, it brought an opportunity. As the bombs fell, huge craters were created around the camp, and one such hole appeared next to the perimeter fence where we were held.

This was our big chance. Norman McLean and I saw that the crater was deep enough to allow us to crawl under the fence. I went first, but once Norman was clear, too, we heard a shout. 'Hey, c'mon, give us a hand!' We looked over and two other POWs had followed us. They seemed to be struggling, but we managed to pull them out. Both were Americans, Dick Bridges and Glenn Loveland.

As the four of us ran for our lives, Norman thought it would make sense for us to split up. He thought there would be less chance of us getting caught if we divided into two pairs. And that's what happened. Norman and I stayed together, and the Americans went their way.

After three years living under Nazi rule, I hoped that I had finally managed to escape the enemy's iron grip. But, if that was to be the case, it had come at a huge cost in terms of suffering to others: hundreds of lives had been lost or ruined by the bombing. That was hard to come to terms with. In truth, we had no choice but to put that to one side and to try to make sure that our freedom lasted not just for the next few hours, but for a lifetime.

# Following the Red Star

After fleeing Zemun, we carried on running and running. We reached what we thought was a forest on the outskirts of Belgrade, but the ground was so wet that it resembled a swamp. Here we met up again, totally coincidentally, with the Americans, Dick Bridges and Glenn Loveland. The four of us then decided to go on with each other, as a group. By the morning we found a dry spot and waited there to catch our breath. But there were insects crawling everywhere and flying around. They looked very similar to mosquitoes, and the little blighters were biting chunks out of us. On our legs, there were leeches. Thankfully, we all wore long trousers, so they were stuck to the material, rather than the skin of our legs.

We walked for several days, without food, and without knowing if we were going in the right direction, either. In the distance we could see a building, a house. I thought I could see soldiers outside as well. I told the others that it could be a guardhouse, and that we needed to tread carefully. But they thought I was being too cautious. They felt we should carry on, and try to aim for the shelter of another forest we could see in the distance. After a while, we reached that forest, but it was there that one of the boys thought he could hear a noise behind us, as if we were being followed. He was right. And they were only a few hundred yards away. We needed to find cover, and quickly.

Soon we heard shots, four or five of them, in rapid succession. And as our pursuers advanced, we heard more gunfire. We managed to find a little place to duck down, and hid there. The soldiers were now to our right. They kept on firing, but walked by without seeing us. A couple of the boys thought it was safe to go on now. But I warned against that. I thought we had probably just seen the advance party, and feared more would follow very soon. The others took heed of my warning, and we stayed put. True enough, within a couple of minutes a second group of soldiers went past, again without seeing us. Another close shave.

The four of us got on well with each other. I've already mentioned Norman McLean's attributes, and the two Americans were equally brave souls. Dick Bridges was a pilot who had been captured by the Nazis after his plane was shot down. He was physically strong and a deep thinker. An intelligent and genial man, there was no doubting the strength of his conviction. Glenn Loveland was in the US Air Force as well. He, too, was very easy to get along with. It was obvious that Glenn had great respect for Dick, and as the younger of the two, he would depend on his compatriot for advice and guidance.

For days, we carried on walking through rural northern Yugoslavia. Without the use of a compass, we were generally following our noses and our instincts, without really knowing where we were heading. But as time passed, we grew tired and hungry. We decided we would have to go down to one of the villages to get something to eat and drink. 'Dai, you'd better go down and have a look what's in this place because you speak German,' said one of the boys. How German was going to be of any use to me in a rural Yugoslavian village, I don't know. But, such was my need for food and water, I headed for the village without trying to argue the toss.

As I neared a collection of houses, I came across a middle-aged man walking towards me. I stopped and tried out some German on him. He looked at me blankly. Then I said I was a British soldier, and his eyes lit up immediately. 'I speak English,' he said. 'I spent many years working on the prairies in Canada and I picked up some English when I was over there.'

He asked me what I was doing in the village, and I said I was with three other Allied soldiers, and we were hoping to have something to eat and drink, after several days walking through the countryside. He instructed me to go back and fetch the other three, and all four of us walked back into the village. We were welcomed with open arms. Very soon we were given food, water and a chance to wash. There was even mention of us being given shelter in an outbuilding for a few days. But, within no time, those plans were quashed. The man who spoke English rushed towards me, and I knew something was wrong.

'I'm sorry,' he said. 'But you'll have to go. One of our people has gone down to the next village, and he's probably telling someone down there that you're here. So it's not safe for you to stay any longer. But, don't worry, I'll get someone to help you find your way so that you can move on from here.'

Within minutes, a young boy came over, no older than 14 or 15. He was going to show us the way out of the village. He ended up walking with us for quite a while. Once we got to the outskirts of another village a couple of miles away, he left us, assuring us that this was a safe place. And, in this village, in the Fruška Gora area, about 70 miles north-east of Belgrade, we came across the Partisans.

The Partisans were one of the military groups which had been formed to resist the Nazi threat to overcome Yugoslavia. They were led by a man called Josip Broz, or Tito, as he was better known. Since the end of 1943, the British had been supplying the Partisans with arms, so they were very keen to welcome us. But the man who led the local faction of the Partisan army told us it wasn't safe to stay in the village overnight because enemy troops had been seen combing the mountainous Fruška Gora region at the time.

Consequently, many local people were planning to leave the area, and move to a safer place. We were instructed to go with them. A large group of us gathered, I'm not sure how many exactly, but there were scores of us. Partisan soldiers, local people – men, women and children – with horses and carts, and four Allied soldiers who were on the run. We were told that we would have to walk through the night. I can't say that I was looking forward to the prospect. After all, we had just walked for days after fleeing Zemun, and now we were on the move again. But it was a case of needs must, and I knew that we had no other option.

The very moment darkness descended we were on our way. But, unfortunately, as we began our trek, the heavens opened, and down came the rain. As we looked to the sky, we could see the German aeroplanes circling above us. This was the last thing we needed. The rain, torrential though it was, didn't pose a real threat, but a potential air attack was a totally different matter. We carried on regardless, and were soon relieved to see the planes pass by.

As we carried on walking, I grew more and more tired. The days on the run from Zemun were catching up with me. My legs were like lead, at the point of seizing up. I told Norman, Dick and Glenn I would have to stop.

'My legs are just giving up on me boys,' I said. 'The next time we stop, wherever that will be, that will be the end of the road for me.'

'No way, Dai,' said one of them. 'You can't give up now. You've got to carry on.'

The next thing I knew we came to a railway line. The Partisans instructed us all to sit down. 'Quiet, everyone,' the leader said. 'Don't move at all. Keep absolutely still and silent.'

And for a few seconds, there was an eerie silence. Then, all of a sudden, we heard the unmistakable chatter of machine gun fire.

I can't really explain what happened next. But, from almost giving up a few minutes earlier – at the point of exhaustion – I summoned some strength from somewhere. I jumped up and ran as fast as I could over the railway line, as the others had. And, after crossing the railway, we knew we were nearing safer ground. We were within half a mile of the Bosut forest. The area was a stronghold for the Partisans, those soldiers who wore a special badge on their caps, the symbol of the 'Red Star'. And from now on, I would be wearing that cap as well.

# Bullets and Screams

We walked for several hours and arrived at a village where we met up with yet another local Partisan faction leader. He said the four of us would be given accommodation in the village, but in separate houses.

I was taken to a very traditional-looking house, and though it was pretty basic inside, it was also clean. An elderly man and woman lived there, and they welcomed me in with smiling faces. A sizeable cauldron was placed in the middle of the room, filled to the brim with water. My Partisan friend told me to strip and get in the pot. It was bath time, a luxury I hadn't been afforded for quite some time. As the others turned their backs, I took my clothes off and left them on a seat, and the elderly man and woman took them to be washed.

Washed, dried and refreshed, I made it to my room by candlelight. I hadn't slept in a proper bed for a while. As I got in, all kinds of thoughts swept into my mind. Was it safe for me to be there? Would the family let the Nazis know I was there? Could I trust them? Those doubts gave way to tiredness, and I soon I fell asleep. I slept like a log.

Next morning, I awoke to the sound of chatter and laughing. From the safety of my blankets, I looked up and saw there were two other beds in the room, and there were three girls there, in their late teens or early twenties, presumably the daughters of the house. But I couldn't get out of bed with these girls in the same room as me. I had slept naked, and I didn't have my own clothes to hand because they were being washed. I was stranded, so I tightened my grip on the blankets, much to the amusement of the three girls! Fortunately my blushes were spared, as the lady of the house soon returned with my clothes, clean and dried. I later discovered that I had actually been sleeping in the bed which was normally occupied by the pair whose house it was. They had shown me great kindness, not only providing me with my bed and board, but giving up their own bed so I could have a good night's sleep.

The Partisans had warned us that on no account were we to tell anyone who we were or where we'd come from. There were two reasons for that. Firstly, if the local people didn't know anything about us, then they couldn't pass any information on to the enemy, either by accident or design.

Secondly, it was important to protect those people who allowed us to stay at their homes, because if the enemy knew we had been there, they could be in serious trouble.

In the morning we had breakfast with the family. Because I didn't speak their language, conversation was difficult, if not impossible. But the Partisan who was with me did speak with the three daughters. As they chatted away, there were hoots of laughter every now and again.

Later, I got to know what the source of this merriment was. Apparently, the girls had been telling the Partisan that only three nights before our visit, a German officer – not an ordinary soldier – had slept in the same bed as I had! So, the Germans were never far away.

The food was tasty, and there was plenty of it. I felt revitalised. The other three had been treated well also. But one of the Americans had inadvertently given away a few personal details. This was a mistake. When the Partisans got wind of this, we knew full well what was going to happen next. We would be on the move, and pretty sharpish. A few miles up the road we stayed in another village, and after a few days there, we were on the move again. This became a pattern of life with the Partisans, and we had to get used to it.

I remember in one of the villages Norman McLean and I went for a bit of a wander. After we had walked a while, Norman decided he was tired and wanted forty winks. He had only lain down and shut his eyes for a few seconds, when he sprang back up. I'd never seen Norman move so quick. Not many things scared Norman, but this experience was clearly one of the exceptions. As he slept, a snake had slithered across his face. I don't think it was poisonous; I would say it was some kind of grass-snake. But, it was enough to wake Norman up and give him one hell of a fright.

We had enjoyed the hospitality of several villages by now. What we didn't know however was that over the two weeks or so we had been living with the Partisans, one of them had been keeping a very close eye on us. He was a short man, early to mid twenties, with an easy way about him. But he always carried a gun. One day, however, out of the blue, he told us that he was leaving. He shook hands with all four of us, and off he went. We were then joined by another man, Otto, who had been a professor at the University in Belgrade before the war. I asked Otto why the young man with the gun had left us after sticking so close by us over the previous two weeks. Otto said the man had been assigned to us from the very first day we came into contact with the Partisans, for a very specific reason.

He spoke calmly, but the message was chilling. 'If any of you had said a bad word about the Partisans or betrayed them in any way then there is one thing you can be absolutely sure about – that young man would have shot you dead.'

It seems that a couple of weeks before we had come across the Partisans, a German soldier had come to them, claiming he was a deserter who had turned his back on the Nazis. But, a few days later, it seems the German had disappeared, and no one appeared to know what had happened to him. Whatever the truth was about the mystery of the soldier's disappearance, one thing was clear: you crossed the Partisans at your peril.

After another few days on the road, we came to a village which had quite clearly been destroyed. Buildings had been flattened, many had been set on fire. This was the enemy's work, and the Partisans wanted to make sure they wouldn't return. There was a little bridge on the outskirts of the village, crossing a small river. One night we joined the Partisans to help them blow up the bridge, not completely, but enough to ensure enemy vehicles could not cross.

The next day, Norman McLean and I went over to have a look at the bridge. Whilst we made our way over, someone started firing at us. Both of us threw ourselves to the ground instantly. As we were near the river, there were some reeds which offered us some much needed cover. Norman and I stayed there for a while, but we knew from the shots that whoever was firing wasn't far away. We could see some trees in the distance, and we thought we would probably be safe if we could reach them. So we ran, in separate directions and following different routes. After lung-bursting sprints we both managed to reach the cover of the trees safely. But there was no doubt, it had been a close shave, and our hearts were pounding.

When we got back to the village, and told the others what had happened we were given quite a telling-off. And it was deserved. By wandering off, we had put ourselves, and others, possibly, in danger. We were back safely, but it could so easily have been different. We had learned an important lesson.

Having said that, there were other scares as well. One day we heard a heavy vehicle approaching, and we knew by the very sound of it that it belonged to the enemy. We ran to hide behind a ruined house. From there, we could see that it was a small German tank. A soldier came out and went to pee against a wall. We couldn't move an inch, because even the sound of the tiniest displaced stone would have been enough to alert the soldier of our presence. After what seemed an age, he finished what he had to do and went back to his tank. And off he went. What a relief – for us and him! But it was that kind of area: the Germans were never far away, and we had to be constantly on our guard.

Gradually we also learnt more about our fellow travellers. One day Norman and I found ourselves in the company of Otto, the university professor, and one of the Partisan soldiers. The Partisan couldn't speak much English, but he told Otto that we were close to his home village, and he wanted to show Norman and me where he used to live. The name of the village was Sremska Rača, and it had been burned to the ground during the war.

As we approached Sremska Rača, the Serbian suddenly ran to a corner of a nearby field. We could hear his screams; he was crying like a baby and he fell to his knees as if to pray. It was a pitiful sight. We didn't know what we should do. And it got worse. Through his tears, he was trying to tell us something, but, frustratingly, we couldn't understand a word. It really was a heart-breaking experience.

When we got back to where we were staying, I told Otto what had happened. He said he would talk to the Partisan to try to find out what was wrong.

'I took them to where my wife has been buried,' the Partisan told Otto, in Serbian. He then went on to relate the details of the German raid on his village.

If ever a story illustrated the savage cruelty of war, the inhuman depths of mankind, it was this man's testimony. Maybe I shouldn't be sharing it. You may not want to hear it.

Apparently, the soldier's wife was pregnant when enemy forces entered Sremska Rača. She was captured, and while she was still alive, they took the baby from her womb. It was a boy. Worse still, the Partisan said, the baby was castrated by enemy troops. Both mother and son died. In all, it's claimed around 350 villagers were killed during the raid on Sremska Rača.

I just didn't know how to react after hearing about this tragedy. What could I say to this poor Partisan? I had seen this man's emotional suffering at close quarters, and although I couldn't imagine what he was going through, I could understand perfectly now why he reacted as he did.

The route of my wartime journey.

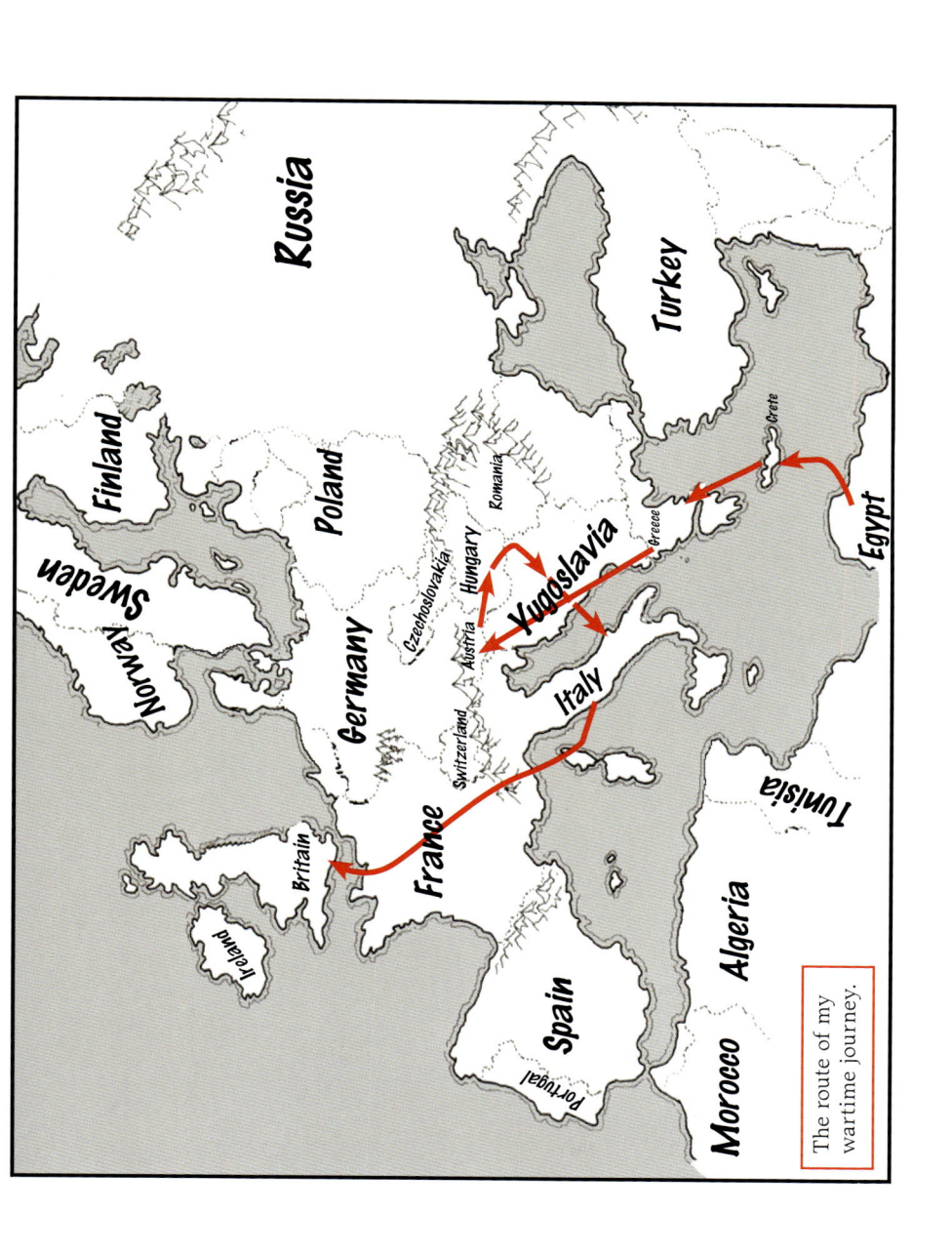

The camp at Zemun, Belgrade in the old Yugoslavia – hell on earth.

Inmates at Zemun, the concentration camp where I was held in spring 1944. I shudder to think what their fate was. It is from here that I managed to escape to the Partisans in April of that year.

The daredevil himself, Norman McLean from Canada.

American pilot Dick Bridges, one of the three who escaped with me from Zemun before going on to fight for the Partisans in Serbia.

Glenn Loveland, another American, who escaped from Zemun with Dick Bridges, Norman McLean and me.

At the end of the war, weighing only seven-and-a-half stones.

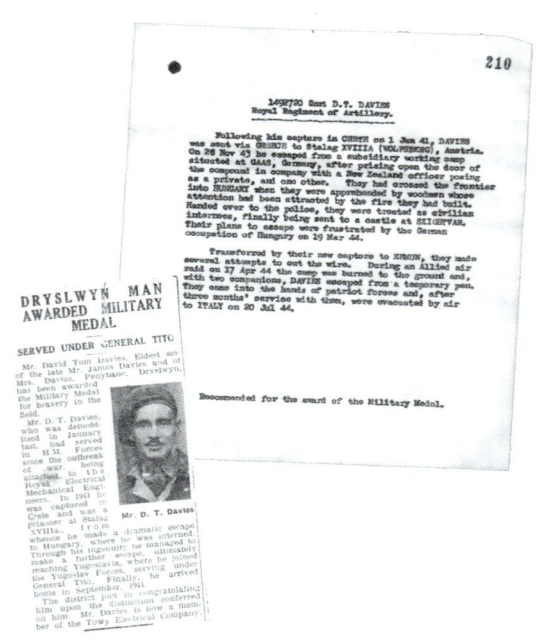

The official citation for the Military Medal, and an associated local newspaper article.

Gurnos Jones from Felingwm as a young soldier. In 2001 we both received medals from the Greek government, 60 years after the Battle of Crete.

*Photo: Aled Llywelyn*

Beti and I pose for the camera on our wedding day in 1954.

My sons, Graham, Michael and Andrew, with me on the square in Murau, Austria, where I was a prisoner in 1942. Going back was a strange experience.

With Herr Mosshammer, whose father, Franz, had been one of our supervisors whilst we were prisoners in Murau.

Outside a hotel in Murau with Franz Mosshammer's son. He came to meet me because the hotel owners (also pictured) had informed him that I was in town and hoping to track down some of the families of those locals I had got to know as a prisoner of war 70 years earlier.

*Photo: Ioan Wyn Evans*

A red letter day. Beti and I are joined by Dr Brinley Jones and his wife Stephanie on the day that I was made a fellow of University of Wales, Trinity St David.

One big happy family.
*Back row, left to right*: Llew (Michael's son), Liz (Andrew's wife), Tom (Andrew's son), Morgan (Michael's daughter), Andrew (my son), Michael (my son), Graham (my son).
*Middle row*: Sara (Ann's daughter), Maddy (Andrew's daughter), Ella (Andrew's daughter), Lisa (Ann's daughter), Mara (Michael's wife), Ann (my daughter).
*Front row*: Myself and Betty

Presenting a wreath at Galatas in May 2016 to mark the 75th anniversary of the Battle of Crete.

Meeting with Michael Fallon MP, the Defence Secretary (left), and talking about the importance of commemorating the Battle of Crete.

Addressing the crowd at the Welch Regiment Memorial at Galatas.

May 2016. Beti and me, arm in arm with some of the Maori contingent at the 75th anniversary of the Battle of Crete.

A poignant family moment for me at the Welch Regiment Memorial at Galatas, with (from left to right) Andrew, Graham, Beti and Michael.

Unity between the generations. Many schoolchildren attended the events to mark the 75th anniversary of the Battle of Crete, and I found this most touching.

Beti and me today. *Photo: Aled Llywelyn*

# A Flight to Freedom

Keeping on the move was a key tactic for the Partisans. They believed the combination of uncertainty and surprise kept them one step ahead of the enemy. One day we were in an open spot, surrounded by an area of forest. It was a hot day, and we had taken some of our clothes off and hung them on a hedge to give them a bit of an airing. It was a chance to enjoy the weather and relax a little. But during our time with the Partisans we had come to realise that quiet periods rarely lasted long. And so it was that day.

Out of the blue we heard the noise of a small aeroplane. Looking up, we saw a Stork, or a *Storch* to give it its correct name. Like a bird of prey, it circled above us menacingly. We knew from experience how the Stork operated: it would hang in the air for a short while then move away, before returning again suddenly and unexpectedly. There was something about the sound of its engine: we couldn't hear it until it was right above us, and that made it a potent attacker. Word had it that some of the Stork pilots switched off their engine for a few seconds and let the plane drop a bit, before firing it up again. Whether that was true or not, it was a plane that took the enemy by surprise.

True to form, after a period of flying above us, then going away, it came back again a few minutes later. And when it came back, it dropped grenades. We heard some minor explosions as those landed several hundred yards away in the forest. But, thankfully, on this occasion the Stork was off-target, and we all breathed a huge sigh of relief as it turned away, and didn't return.

We very often felt quite exposed with the Partisans, because there was a distinct shortage of weapons, and defending ourselves could be a problem. A few days after the Stork attack, we had a message that we should expect an airdrop. A plane would come with supplies and arms for the Partisans. The aircraft wasn't going to land. It would drop its cargo using parachutes, and we were instructed to collect everything as it fell to the ground in nearby fields.

By this time, we could send out radio signals as well. We did do this by using a bicycle and a small generator. The bike would be turned upside down, and someone would turn the pedals, critically at a constant speed, to generate enough power for the message to be transmitted. By today's high-tech standards it all sounds very old fashioned, laughable even, but we had to make the best of what we had at the time.

A few days after the first cargo landed another one arrived with more supplies. This consignment included something called a PIAT gun. (I think it stood for Projector, Infantry, Anti Tank gun.) It arrived in the biggest box I've ever seen. But, it was in bits, and it needed to be assembled. When the Partisans opened the box, they saw a chunky book of instructions. But they hardly understood a word: it was all in English. So, I was summoned to read the instructions and help with the onerous task of assembling this monster of a gun.

After several frustrating hours, scratching our heads and shouting the odd choice word, we did manage to get the job done. The PIAT was quite a powerful gun. It would shoot little rockets, rather than bullets, and it had enough armoury to stop a small tank in its tracks. But, before using it, of course, practice was required. I was again called upon to read the English instructions, and after relaying those to the ones doing the firing, with copious use of hand signals, we were ready to try it out.

As the rockets were loaded, the anticipation and tension built. Because of a mixture of nervousness and excitement, the soldier in charge of the gun pulled the trigger without looking properly where he was firing. The rocket crashed into a pig sty. Luckily, the Partisan soldier's elementary mistake didn't turn out to be a fatal one, and no one was killed or injured. The pig was happily rolling in a nearby field at the time, completely oblivious to the fact that its sleeping quarters had been unceremoniously destroyed. But at least we knew now that the PIAT gun was in full working order!

Many of the Partisans' military activities happened at night, under the cover of darkness. I remember one occasion when they had gone to a flour mill nearby, which was guarded by enemy troops. We weren't with them that night but, when they got back, we heard what had happened. The Partisans had managed to get their hands on some supplies of flour, but it was at a cruel cost. One of the leaders of the local faction, a blacksmith by trade, and a very popular and good-looking young man, had been shot and killed. The next morning a cloud of despair hung over the whole area. Although I'd only known the man briefly, such was the collective feeling of grief, I felt as if I'd lost a member of my own family. And it certainly was a massive blow to the Partisan 'family' locally to lose a man of such charisma and conviction.

Three nights after the young leader's death, the Partisans captured three enemy soldiers and brought them back with them. According to what we were told, these men had played key roles in raids on local villages where scores of people had been killed and buildings destroyed. The attacks were completely indiscriminate, we were told. Killings had been made in cold blood and homes set on fire, without knowing if their occupants supported the Partisans or not. The fact that these people lived in an area where the Partisans were active seemed to provide the enemy with enough justification to perpetrate their cruel attacks.

Anyway, we didn't really know what the Partisans were going to do with these three men who had been captured. They would obviously try to get information from them about plans for future enemy attacks, and so forth. But, beyond that, we didn't know what the fates of these men would be.

The Partisans were ahead of their time in a way, because

## A Flight to Freedom

their forces included a high percentage of female recruits. There were reports of as many as 100,000 women fighting in Tito's army during the war.

The three captured men were paraded in front of onlookers, and although we couldn't really follow what was being said, we sensed the tension and we knew things were very close to boiling point. Suddenly, one of the women soldiers leapt to her feet. All Partisan soldiers routinely carried a knife, and the woman walked over to three captured men with a large knife in her hand. She grabbed one of the men's hair and pulled his head right back. I thought she was going to slit his throat there and then. But at that very moment there was a shout from an officer, and the woman soldier took a step back. A group of Partisans marched in and took the three men with them. What happened to the three? I don't know, but we never saw them again.

People can do the strangest things in times of war, and there were reports of cruelty orchestrated by the Partisans as well. I must say I always found them to be fair, but I was on their side, of course, and living amongst them. However, when they were angered I could see how fiery they could become, and I sensed they were fearless people. Absolutely fearless.

Although arms and supplies had been flown in from Britain, there was still a shortage of general goods and materials. My army issue boots were absolutely ruined after being on the run, and boots were in scant supply amongst the Partisans generally. In wartime having solid footwear was important, almost as essential as being properly armed. But, you'll never believe what I had on my feet. In Wales, before the war, we used to 'pork a pig'. After we had killed it, we would leave the skin on the meat, removing only the hair. In Yugolsavia, they did things differently. They would take the skin off completely, and then hang and dry the skin. And that's what I had on my feet: a pair of pig skin shoes. They were more like slippers, really, some kind of moccasins. They didn't fit properly, and they weren't the sturdiest, but they were better than nothing.

It wasn't a time when we could pick and choose, in terms of things to wear or food to eat. We had to make do with what we had, or what we could get. I remember one day when we went to one of these ruined villages, Dick Bridges, the American pilot who was in our group of POWs, wandered around a building which had been partly destroyed and found a chimney stack still intact. There was a kind of shelf built into the chimney, and Dick put his hand on the shelf, just above his head, and a pulled a small square block from it. It looked like a brick. Dick cleaned it, and realised it was a lump of lard, pig lard. We took it back with us and ate it. It was a case of 'waste not, want not'.

Later we came across a disused hay barn. I think whoever had used it had been growing a type of sweet corn. Dick and his fellow American, Glenn Loveland, found some corn on the cob in the barn. And they brought us a few. I told the boys not to touch them. I was sure mice or rats had been at them.

'No, Dai. They're fine. There's nothing wrong with

them,' they said. The two Americans went ahead to gather some wood and light a fire, and to heat the corn. They then shared it between us. And there it was: popcorn. It was the very first time I'd tasted it and I was doing so outside an old hay barn in Yugoslavia, all courtesy of two American airmen!

Many of the villages we passed through revered the Orthodox Church. On the outside their churches looked very simple and ordinary, but inside they were very different. Many had stunningly intricate murals of religious icons adorning the walls, not to mention other examples of ornate craftsmanship in every nook and cranny.

In one village we met the local priest. It was difficult to know his age, but he had a long grey beard and wore a full-length black silk gown, as was the norm for an Orthodox priest. He wanted to show us his church. We followed him in only to be faced with a most distressing sight. The place had been defaced and ravaged. Someone had drawn and written indecent slogans on the sacred images. And at the altar there were deposits of faeces and the unmistakable stench of urine. The priest was in tears as he told us enemy troops were responsible for these gross acts when they stormed through the village. He was a broken man. All this had been done in the name of war. I couldn't make sense of it. It was another terrible example of mankind sinking to unfathomable depths.

As the conflict prolonged in the Balkans, the Partisan military campaign grew ever more dependent on having efficient supplies of arms and equipment. Despite the parachute drops, there was always a chance that the supplies didn't land where they should, or that the enemy could get their hands on them. The upshot was that we needed to find a decent place where the cargo planes could actually touch down and land. We found somewhere which fitted the bill in the Morovič area. As the planes would land in the dark, we needed to light a fire which was big enough for the pilot to see, to guide him down from the sky. We did that, but soon we came under enemy fire. They had obviously seen the bonfire and we had to abort the plan.

Soon after there was another parachute drop of arms and equipment. Amongst the supplies that came down were some gooseneck lamps. We used these, rather than the large distracting bonfires, to help guide cargo plane pilots. We placed these at different spots to show him where the landing should begin and end. The system worked well, and we managed to access all the cargo without much trouble.

We were then informed that 25 wounded and injured Partisans were supposed to go back on the aeroplane, to have hospital treatment. But only 20 of the Partisans had come. The other five had been held up somewhere, and the pilot was getting was growing more irate by the waiting minute. 'Look, I can't wait any longer,' he said. 'It's too dangerous. I really can't wait. I have to go.'

Then, completely unexpectedly, one of the Partisan soldiers who was with us turned to one of the British officers, who had accompanied the pilot, and said that I suffered constantly with malaria. I should take one of the spare places on the plane, he said.

'Fine,' said the officer, looking towards us. 'You five! In you go!'

I really couldn't believe what I was hearing. I stepped up on to the plane as if I was in a trance. As I looked behind me, I could see my friends following me. There they were: the Canadian, Norman McLean, the two American airmen, Dick Bridges and Glenn Loveland, the four of us who had escaped together from the concentration camp at Zemun. And there was a fifth. Sammy Hoare – the New Zealander who was with us in Hungary – had rejoined us recently, after fleeing to be with the Partisans.

Without warning, the five of us had all been granted tickets on a plane to freedom. On 20 July, 1944, we flew from Yugoslavia to Bari in southern Italy. Unexpected and unplanned, but quite typical of the way things happened in wartime, it was the sweetest experience imaginable. On that summer night, Lady Luck had shone her light on me.

# Home Again

When we reached Bari there were questions galore. The five of us were interviewed separately for quite some time by Allied army officers, which was understandable. They needed to verify that we weren't imposters and that we were telling the truth. There was a danger, after all, that we could have been spies. But, luckily, all five of us managed to convince our inquisitors that we were the people we claimed to be.

After the paperwork had been done, we were provided with a military escort from Bari in south-east Italy, right across the country to Napoli (Naples) in the south-west. It was quite a journey, about 165 miles.

When we got to Naples, the American authorities arrived to meet Dick Bridges and Glenn Loveland and take them to their base. Then, Canadian officers came to escort Norman McLean, followed by representatives from the New Zealand army, who collected Sammy Hoare. There was only one man left.

The malaria had returned to bother me once more, so I was taken to the city's American hospital to be treated. I spent a few days there before being moved to Salerno, about 70 miles south of Naples. At a convalescence home there I had a chance to recover and recuperate. At the time I only weighed seven-and-a-half stone. I was scrawny and weak. The war had taken its toll.

After almost five years overseas, I arrived back in Britain in September 1944. What a strange feeling that was. As I got on the train at Liverpool, bound for Cardiff, I started to worry. One of the main things that concerned me was how I would react when someone spoke to me in Welsh. In the years I'd been away, I'd had no real chance to speak the language for any length of time. I'd come across Welsh people who were POWs, but they didn't speak Welsh. It was strange, because in the time I'd been away, I had learned quite a bit of German, and grew to speak it reasonably fluently. But I hadn't any chance to use my Welsh, and that really worried me.

On the train my mind was buzzing with imaginary conversations in Welsh, and I grew frustrated when I couldn't remember certain words. I got as far as Carmarthen without hearing a single word of Welsh. And then when I stepped on the bus which would take me home to Dryslwyn, the conductor looked at me and said, *'Wel, bachan, wy' ddim wedi dy weld ti ers sbel. Ble ti 'di bod?'* Or, in English, 'Well, boy, I haven't seen you for a while. Where have you been?' To hear that simple greeting in my native language really touched me. I knew now I was home. I opened my mouth to answer the conductor, and the words just came from somewhere. It was as if I'd never been away.

After a period of home leave, I was posted to the Royal Technical College in Glasgow. I was there to train to become an army radio operator. Whilst I was in Scotland, I heard I'd been nominated for the Military Medal, in recognition of my wartime service. It was quite a shock, and I honestly didn't expect it because I thought I was only doing what I'd been called up to do. But, of course, to be awarded the medal was a huge honour.

In December 1944 I was supposed to go down to London to be presented with the MM by King George VI. But my old enemy, the malaria, had returned yet again. So I had to make do with a presentation from a Colonel in Glasgow. Although I never got to meet the King, several decades later I did shake his daughter's hand when I was presented with the OBE.

After the war ended, I found it very difficult to settle back home in Dryslwyn. My parents were there, but most of my old friends had moved away to find work. I had come home to a very different village from the one I'd known before the war. Before I left the army, I had been offered the chance to become a full-time professional soldier. At the time I rejected the opportunity, because I felt I'd had enough of regimented military life. But, after a few months at home, I did start to think once more about re-joining the army.

Settling back into civilian life, particularly in a quiet, rural area was a challenge. Of course, I'd spent three years as a prisoner of war, and seen many awful things. And there were other, simpler, more practical factors which affected everyday life as well.

Rural Wales, and particularly Carmarthenshire, was

famous for its hospitality. And in my area, every household was welcoming and generous. That's the way it was. If I called anywhere, at someone's house or at a farm, they wouldn't allow me to leave without providing a huge meal – meat, potatoes and all kinds of vegetables. There would be a mountain of food on the plate. And my stomach couldn't cope with that. I'd gone for years as a POW living on tiny amounts of food and water. So, for several years after the war, I could only tackle a very modest plate of food. I spent years trying to politely decline the kind of offer of food, and hoping the refusal wouldn't cause any offence.

For many who had left the armed forces at the end of war, trying to secure a full-time job could also be a problem. I was lucky, though. An old school friend, Eirwyn Thomas, worked as an electrician. He did a lot of work in the London area, and he offered the chance for me to go with him. I took that up, and we worked in London for six months or more. Then an opportunity came to return to our home area. It was the time when electricity was beginning to reach every corner of the country, and we were given a contract to wire our local chapel. We worked at a church nearby as well, and other contracts soon followed. In 1947 Eirwyn and I set up a company - Towy Electrical – and I ran the business for 40 years before selling it on. The company still exists, although I'm no longer part of it.

In rural Wales, the period after the war saw the growth of the Young Farmers' Clubs. They were an important social organisation in our area and beyond. And over the years so many couples went on to marry after meeting at YFC get-togethers that the organisation developed a reputation as a very effective if unofficial dating agency. And so it was for me. I became involved with the local YFC and one of our members was a young lady called Beti. Fortunately, she spotted something in me, and I saw much more in her. We got married in 1954, and throughout the years Beti has been my rock. We've enjoyed a very happy and contented life together. We've had four children – Michael, Graham, Andrew and Ann. Michael has just retired after a long career as a doctor, practising as a GP over the border in Herefordshire. Graham is a Professor in Clinical Chemistry at King's in London. Until he retired recently, Andrew was the Director of Commercial Services for Merlin Entertainments, who run various attractions across the world, including Madame Tussauds and Legoland. Ann is the last of the brood, and she has chosen to stay in the area. She lives next door to us in Dryslwyn and works for the local authority, Carmarthenshire County Council. Beti and I are very proud of them all. We have seven grandchildren as well, and, naturally, we take great delight in what they've all achieved so far in their young lives.

As our children got older, some people in the area pressed me to stand for election as a local councillor. I must admit that the idea didn't appeal to me at all when it was first mooted. But, after a bit of coaxing, at the eleventh hour I put my name forward, and was elected as a county councillor for Carmarthenshire County Council in 1970. With the re-organisation of local authorities, Dyfed County Council was established in 1974, amalgamating the three old counties of Carmarthenshire, Pembrokeshire and Ceredigion. I was a sitting member until another re-organisation in 1996. Then, when Carmarthenshire County Council was re-established, I served as a councillor until I retired in 2003. During the decades I was involved in local government I was fortunate enough to be Chairman of Dyfed County Council in 1981-82, and to be appointed the first Chairman of Carmarthenshire County Council for two years, after the re-organisation of 1996.

Despite my initial doubts about putting myself up for election, I enjoyed my years as a councillor immensely. I did get a lot of satisfaction from trying to help people in my community. Of course I didn't always succeed, but I always tried, and I think people value that at least. And, strange as it may seem, I've no doubt that my wartime experiences as a POW helped me perform my duties as a councillor. That period showed me how important it was to listen and think before reacting or saying something. I feel those are elementary skills for any councillor. I also think that what I saw during the war taught me humility, hopefully. I realised how important it was to consider the views of other people and the situations in which they found themselves as well. No one knows everything. We can all learn from each other, and we should listen to all voices, particularly those who shout the least, and often have no voice. As a councillor, it was always my mission to treat everyone in exactly the same way, whatever their background – and I think that is a trait I picked up from my time as a POW as well.

The war also strengthened my belief in democracy. After all, fighting against the extremist ideas of a dictator was the reason for going to war in the first place. And, county councils were built on the idea that local decisions should be made democratically. That is why I don't like the current cabinet system which exists within local authorities, where ten to a dozen people effectively decide what should happen on all the important matters. To me, that is not democracy. The voice of the local councillor can no longer be heard, and that defeats the objective of electing someone to represent the interests of the people in the first place. In my view, introducing the cabinet system has been the most damaging innovation in local government.

Above all else, the war taught me the importance of working with other people, from different backgrounds, beliefs and nations. 'In unity, there is strength,' according to the old saying. And I've always believed in that. I found, personally, that in times of trouble I had to place my trust in a group of people, and we all came together to pull in the same direction. Those men who escaped with me shared my belief in the right to freedom. And that has been integral to my philosophy on life: without freedom, we have nothing.

The years which followed the end of the war were very different times to those we live in nowadays, where technology and computers have made the world a much smaller place. After the war people in different parts of the world didn't really communicate with each other because keeping in touch was simply not as easy as it is today.

Consequently, I lost contact with the people I'd grown to trust most as we fled from the enemy's grasp. But, decades after the war ended, I did manage to find out – by accident more than design sometimes – what had happened to most of the men who had escaped with me.

# Past and Present

The Greek island of Crete was where I was first captured and became a prisoner of war. And every year, at the end of May, a reunion is held for Allied soldiers who were part of the Battle of Crete in 1941. Over the years, I've attended many of these events. I believe they're very important milestones: an opportunity to remember those who gave their lives in battle. And as someone who survived the rigours of war, I think it's imperative that we commemorate the efforts of those who weren't as fortunate.

I particularly remember one reunion I attended in the late 1980s. At these events, every former soldier has to queue to register on arrival at the cemetery where those killed in battle on the island are buried. My name was called and up I went. And as I was registering, I heard someone shout, 'Gurnos Jones'. Well, I can tell you that although 'Jones' is probably the most common surname in Wales, the first name, 'Gurnos' is very unusual. And when I heard that name, I immediately looked up, because I knew a man with that very name. And there he was, standing there, Gurnos Jones from the village of Felin-gwm in Carmarthenshire – my neck of the woods. Gurnos had been with the Commandos in Crete, and he, too, had been captured. But he had managed to get away, and spent most of the war in Egypt, if I remember correctly. Funnily enough, when we were both in Crete in 1941 we hadn't come across each other, but it was lovely to see him at the reunion several decades later. And in a special ceremony that day, we were both awarded with a medal to recognise our services in Crete. I was obviously proud to receive the medal in any case, but it gave me added pleasure to receive it at the same time as Gurnos, although neither of us knew the other was going to be there.

During the reunion I was one of half a dozen or so former soldiers who were invited by the Prime Minister of Greece at the time to attend a dinner of commemoration. And amongst the other guests was the Duke of Kent, representing the royal family. At the event I got chatting to a former soldier from New Zealand. I told him that I'd spent quite a bit of time in the company of a soldier from New Zealand, and that we'd escaped together from Austria to Hungary. He asked me what the soldier's name was. 'Oh, Roy Natusch,' I said. The New Zealander looked at me, open-mouthed.

'You won't believe this,' he said. 'Roy Natusch is my neighbour!' Well, he was right – I couldn't believe it. Over 40 years after I'd last seen Roy, I had come face to face with his neighbour, on a Greek island. After we'd both had some time to get over the shock, the New Zealander gave me Roy's address. Once I arrived home, I contacted my old mate, and he invited us over to visit. In 1990, Beti and I went out to New Zealand to meet Roy and his family and we had a truly wonderful time in their company.

Roy and I were separated in Hungary in March 1944, but he, too, managed to make it to Yugoslavia. He did so by taking on the persona of a Dutch officer. That was typical of Roy. He was a real character, with a sharp mind and courage to match. It turned out that he had tried to contact me many years before we were reunited. He had come over to Britain, and had made it as far as Swansea, thinking that I lived in the area. He made several enquiries locally to try and find me. He told me he remembered one particular occasion when he went into a shop in Swansea, and said, 'I'm trying to get hold of Dai Davies. Do you know him?' Apparently, the reply from the man behind the counter stopped him in his tracks. 'There's bloody thousands of them around here, butty!'

And that was that. Roy decided that the task of finding me was even beyond his many talents, and he returned to New Zealand thinking we would never see each other again. After the war Roy got married and he and his family farmed for decades in the Hawkes Bay area. He passed away in 2009 aged 90, but I was so grateful that we had been reunited in 1990, and had kept in contact since then. And the wonderful thing is that we've maintained the links with his family, and two of Roy's grandsons have stayed with us at our home in Carmarthenshire. There's no two ways about it, Roy Natusch was a very special man.

I've tried to trace Joe Walker, who escaped with Roy and me from Austria. But, unfortunately, I've had no luck. I last saw him in Hungary in 1944. What happened to him after that, I just don't know.

And what happened to the four others who, like me, were flown out of Yugoslavia in July 1944? I learnt a little about those after the son of one of the Americans contacted me. Tyler Bridges, Dick Bridges' son, is an author and award-winning journalist in the United States. He's also spent quite a bit of time reporting from South America. Whilst researching his father's wartime experiences, he got in touch with me, and I was naturally very pleased to hear from him.

His father died in 2003. The others have passed away as well. Glenn Loveland, another American airman, died in 2009. Both he and Dick were in their 80s. The other two who were with us on that flight to freedom both died relatively young. Norman McLean, the daredevil Commando from Canada was 63, when he passed on in 1979, and Sammy Hoare, the New Zealander, died in 1980, aged 61. I met up with Sammy in London after the war. He married an English girl, and lived in the London area for a while, before returning to his homeland, and it was there that he died.

Earlier, I mentioned a POW called Joe Burke, who fell 30 feet and broke his leg whilst trying to abseil down from a window at Siklós prison in Hungary. I hadn't heard anything of Joe since then. But in 2013 BBC Cymru Wales made a television programme about my wartime escapades for the Welsh-language channel, S4C. The programme was entitiled, *Heb Ryddid, Heb Ddim* ('Without Freedom, We Have Nothing'). After the programme was broadcast, I was contacted by an official from a military association called

The Brotherhood of Veterans of the Greek Campaign. The person who got in touch with me knew of Joe. I was told that he was still alive, and I was given an address for him. Since then, we have sent letters to each other and kept in touch. He lives in the north of England, and is now 96 years old. So, it seems the fall from that high window in Hungary over 70 years ago didn't do any lasting damage!

The TV programme followed me as I returned, accompanied by my three sons, to some of the places I'd been as a POW in Austria. My family didn't know much about my wartime experiences, as it wasn't something I talked about. As I said earlier, it's difficult to describe things to people who weren't there. But my sons obviously wanted to know more, and that's why they were so eager to go with me to Austria. We hadn't arranged much beforehand, but I was keen to visit places like Murau, Sankt Lambrecht and Gaas.

When we arrived in Murau, I knew full well, because of their ages when I got to know them, that Franz Moshammer and Ferdinand Zeiper, the two local men who had showed so much kindness towards us, would have died. But, I wanted to try to find out if their relatives still lived in the area. We enquired in several places in the town, in various shops and offices, but no one seemed to know anything. Then, we were told it might be worth asking the owner of one of the hotels in Murau, as his family had lived in the town for generations and knew the area well.

I went more in hope than expectation, but I was pleasantly surprised. It was great to hear that the hotel owner knew members of both men's families. They still lived locally, and he telephoned them there and then. Within an hour, Franz Moshammer's son and Ferdinand Zeiper's daughter both came to the hotel to meet me. It's hard to put into words, but meeting them was a huge thrill, and it was gratifying to be able to thank them in person for the very honourable way their fathers had treated us as POWs.

I had a similar experience 150 miles away in Gaas, the place where I escaped over the border to Hungary. There we met with the family of Agnes Kraller, the elderly lady who owned the farm where I had worked as a POW. Since meeting her family, my sons have kept in contact with them. And what a lovely feeling that is: to know that the link between the families has been re-established, and hopefully that will continue well into the future.

Whatever anyone thinks about the Nazis and their cruelty, I, and many others, found the ordinary people of Austria to be very fair, kind and supportive. Despite the tensions of war, they showed a respect towards us as POWs, which reaffirmed one's faith in human nature. I will never forget that they treated us with great decency at a time when so many terrible, inhuman acts were witnessed all around us.

# Crete Once More

Returning to Crete has never been difficult for me. Since the 1960s, Beti and I have gone back regularly to attend the reunions to commemorate the Battle of Crete in May 1941. But May 2016 had a particular significance. It was the 75th anniversary, so it was special. It was particularly special because it was the last official reunion for the soldiers who took part in the battle. Over the years, the reunion has been an opportunity for former soldiers from New Zealand, Australia and Britain to meet up to remember those Allied troops who gave their lives on the Greek island. And over the years, naturally, the numbers attending have diminished. This year there were only three of us from Britain, and eight from New Zealand, and many of those were in wheelchairs. The old boys from New Zealand said a while ago that this was going to be their final year attending. After all, making the long plane journey of over 10,000 miles one way is quite a commitment in itself, and as people get older, the travelling gets harder. Some individuals will keep on going, I'm sure, but this year was the last organised reunion, and the last time for me as well, I think.

There was something unique about the commemorations

this year. A different feel. Every village seemed to have organised an event. As much as we would have liked to do so, it was impossible to go everywhere. So, we decided to visit four or five of the key sites and attended the ceremonies at places like Souda Bay, Maleme and Galatas. I was accompanied by Beti, as usual, and my three sons came along as well – and I think that made it even more special time for me. The boys say they will go again, and I hope they do, to continue the family connection with Crete.

All over the island there was great interest in the commemorations. The Cretans had come out in force to show their support. Over the years, Beti and I have made friends with people locally, and one family in particular. They live up in the mountains, and they are lovely people, so kind and friendly, typical Cretans. The son came down to meet us this time. It was funny because he said his mother had become very excited after seeing me on television in one of the ceremonies. The events were covered extensively by Greek TV, and there were cameras everywhere we went.

I've always felt really close to the people of Crete. And I think there was a bond there, from the early days, between us as Allied soldiers and the Cretans. I remember when we first arrived during the war, they were so pleased to see us. We were welcomed as we marched through all the little villages. They were generous, and whenever they could they gave us food, and plenty of moral support.

What I found particularly touching this time was that there were so many schoolchildren attending the events.

Children are taught in school what happened on the island during the war. They recognise our efforts, and they have an understanding of what occurred: it's part of their history. We took photos with the children at the ceremonies, and they really were lovely moments. There was a sense of unity between the generations, and that was very touching.

I think that here in the UK as well, young people are becoming increasingly aware of what happened in the two world wars. There have been several programmes recently commemorating 100 years since some of the major events of the First World War, like the Battle of the Somme. It's helped the young to take an interest, to realise the true horrors of war, but I think it's made them appreciate the sacrifices as well. And most of all, perhaps, it's helped them to understand the importance of freedom, and not to take it for granted.

That was something I was constantly reminded of during the various ceremonies in Crete. We do take things for granted. Very often it was the little things, the simple things, which reminded me of that.

In all the ceremonies, everyone recited the world-famous poem, 'Ode of Remembrance, For the Fallen' by Laurence Binyon:

> They shall grow not old, as we that are left grow old;
> Age shall not weary them, nor the years condemn.
> At the going down of the sun and in the morning,
> We will remember them.

And whilst everyone else was reciting the English version, it was the Welsh translation that was on my lips. And those words hit me every time: 'Ni heneiddiant hwy fel ni a adawyd; / Ni ddwg oed iddynt ludded na'r blynyddoedd gollfarn mwy, / Pan elo'r haul, ac ar wawr y bore, / Ni a'u cofiwn hwy'.

There were Welsh people at several of the ceremonies, particularly the one organised at the Welch Regiment Memorial at Galatas. I don't think that people in Wales realise that so many Welsh soldiers lost their lives in the Battle of Crete – there are 91 buried in one cemetery alone. And many more died. I think that most of the Welsh people who attended the Welch Regiment ceremony were ones who had come to live in Crete. And there are a lot of them there. If only there was a way to raise awareness in Wales itself about the Battle of Crete and the Welsh connection. We need to remember the sacrifice of the fallen soldiers from Wales.

In truth, I would say that people in Britain in general don't know enough about the battle. The UK government Defence Secretary, Michael Fallon, MP, had come out to Crete for the events. I met with him and spoke with him. I thanked him for coming. He said that wasn't necessary. It was his duty, he said, and I was pleased to hear that.

But I think that the reason that the Battle of Crete is largely forgotten is because it was a defeat. We lost. Had we won it would have been different. The Germans suffered huge losses, as we did. But they won the battle. The margins between victory and defeat in these battles can be very slim, and it's a shame that the lost ones generally don't get the same attention, in terms of commemoration, as those where Britain was victorious.

It was good to see the 75th anniversary events in Crete were so well attended. They came from near and far, and there was a strong representation of New Zealand Maoris. At the end of each ceremony a Maori lament was sung. It was simple, but so haunting. It was extremely powerful. Such a moving experience.

On a personal note, I was delighted to be able to attend these events. Being asked to present wreaths in memory of the fallen was a great honour. The very nature of commemorations like these mean they are bitter-sweet. We are remembering and celebrating lives at the same time.

For most of us who took part in the Battle of Crete, the last page in the chapter has been closed. We will not be returning. But, if future generations wish to carry on with the tradition, then that would be a fitting tribute for those who lie in Cretan graves, far from home. 'We will remember them.'

# Lessons Learned?

When I signed up for the army in 1939, I thought it would be for six months, just a relatively short period of military training. But, of course, the six months became six years, and during that time I witnessed some awful scenes, scenes that are impossible to forget. No matter how hard someone tries to banish those kinds of things from the mind, it's not possible to erase everything.

Without a doubt, the Nazi concentration camp in Belgrade, Yugoslavia was the worst place I came across. I witnessed things there that I will never be able to describe, where some cruel people treated their fellow humans in the most inhuman ways. It really did beggar belief. The only way I could deal with what I saw was by concentrating on trying to escape from that god-forsaken place. And that was the only thing on my mind, day and night. To escape and be free. Free from a regime which had sunk to depths I never thought mankind could reach.

Of course, decades later, these scenes of cruelty and despair come back to haunt someone every now and again. Very often they come back when someone is alone with his thoughts, and lets the mind wander. It's strange, but you hear things when it's quiet. Voices from the past. Noises.

And when I think of Zemun, it's the groans. Those groans of pain. Maybe it's not as clear now as it was years ago, but it's still there. Of course, I'm one of the lucky ones, I made it out alive from Zemun. Many others weren't so fortunate. But, after getting out of places like that, you have to try to put the terrible experiences to one side and carry on with life. That's the only way to deal with it.

Sometimes I ask myself if mankind has really learned any lessons from the war. Do people behave any better towards their fellow humans now? When someone thinks of the terrible atrocities which are carried out these days, perpetrated by terrorists who target innocent people, I'm left thinking that things haven't really improved at all. And what worries me more than anything is that we could see a situation developing when we will see another war on a worldwide scale.

I'm a great believer in the axiom that it is better to 'jaw, jaw, rather than war, war'. There is definitely something in that. It's essential that problems are discussed and that people with opposing views talk to each other, in the hope of finding common ground, of finding a solution. But I also believe that everyone has a duty to stand up for their family, their loved ones and what is theirs. I'm not a philosopher of any kind, but I think that when all the avenues for discussion have been closed, then, unfortunately, we have no option but to step up firmly to the breach.

My wartime experiences have undoubtedly left an indelible mark on me. I think that what happened to me and the things I witnessed, together with my upbringing of course, shaped my personality and influenced the rest of my life. In 2014 I was honoured by the University of Wales Trinity St. David, and made an Honorary Fellow. During the ceremony I was asked to address the audience, many of them new, young graduates. The few words I had for them summarise my general philosophy on life.

Firstly, for me, there are three things in life which come above all else. The first is respect. Respect yourself, your families, your friends and your colleagues. Secondly, loyalty. Be loyal to those who need your support – your loved ones, your family, friends and colleagues. And thirdly, practise humility. If you do everything in life with humility then people will respect you and be loyal to you, because of the way you live your life.

I know that some of the acts of shocking cruelty I witnessed have shaken my faith in mankind. I don't profess to be a religious man, but I hope that I follow Christian values in the way that I try to live my life. Christianity teaches us, of course, to forgive people. But, I must confess, I do find it very difficult to forgive people who have committed heinous acts and caused unbelievable suffering. This may sound strange, but it's difficult to convey what cruelty actually is and to describe it. The word *cruelty* conveys some kind of image in people's minds, of course. But, when you're there, and you *see* cruelty meted out in front of your eyes, then that is something totally different.

During the war I also witnessed acts of kindness. Acts of bravery, as well, where people went well beyond the call of duty to help someone else. And, when weighing everything up, I can only hope that there is more good in this world than bad.

So, what about the millions of people who have been killed and injured in wars around the world? Can all the sacrifices made in the name of war be justified? It's a huge question isn't it? But, when someone considers what happened to Jewish people especially during the Second World War, and the extreme cruelty they suffered, then the fight to bring Hitler and his vile empire to its knees *must* have been a just one.

For me, the most important thing is that we remember. Remember those who lost their lives, from every nation across the world; and to remember their sacrifice. I think everyone needs to bear that in mind, people of all ages and backgrounds, but especially the young. Because without the sacrifices of others, where would they be today? Whatever your views on war, it's imperative that we remember those who didn't come home, and my biggest hope is that we will never see anything like it again. Ever.